Published by Elisa's Backporch Design Inc.
1200 Forest Road NW
Albuquerque, NM 87114
www.backporchdesign.com

Written by Elisa Wilson
Photos by Alfred Costanzo unless otherwise noted.
Layout , design and illustration by Focus Advertising, Inc.

ISBN 0-9745622-2-2

Printed in Canada by Friesens
10 9 8 7 6 5 4 3 2 1

I pray that the eyes of your heart may be enlightened, so that you may know what is the hope of His calling, what are the riches of the glory of His inheritance in the saints, and what is the surpassing greatness of His power toward us who believe.
Ephesians 1:18-19a

Dedication

This book is dedicated to my beautiful daughters Alaina and Cassandra. May you continue to grow and blossom into young women who reflect His light from within.

Special Thanks
To Linda Noort who does such a beautiful job of quilting.
To Lori Paolino, Amy Varner, Mary Lucille and Amber Peterson for their creative contributions to this book.

Special thanks to Timeless Treasures, Northcott Silk, Inc. and Marcus Brothers for their fabulous fabrics.

Table of Contents

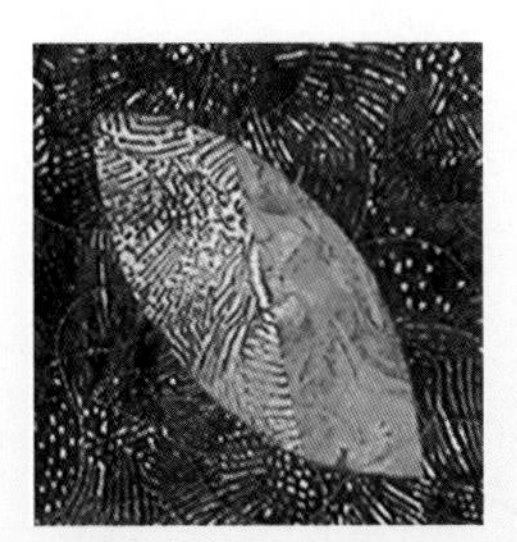

What is the Melon Block?

This block was adapted from a couple of old blocks. You may have seen a similar block called the Melon Patch, Whale Block, Lover's Knot or Spring Beauty. My goal was to incorporate rotary cutting, acrylic templates and easy machine piecing with the charm of these old block patterns. I experimented with many different angles and sizes in order to find the best curve for easy piecing. A corner triangle can be added or a corner square can be to make the Lover's Knot block.

Lines were added to the templates so that you could piece two fabrics together and then cut out your pieces to add more variety to the blocks. You can use the three pieces as they are or by using these lines, add a number of options to make your block more complex. The block itself is not difficult to sew. Don't be afraid to sew curves. I well show you step by step how to make it easy. Using an accurate ¼" seam is extremely important. Be sure to check your machine.

By using the templates and placement lines you have more than a dozen variations. If you add the unlimited amount of fabric colors and choices available, the variety is almost endless.

The book is laid out to show you a sampling of the blocks that you can make. This is to inspire you with a variety of block ideas and fabric choices. You will be shown how to do each step of the block so that if you want to design your own quilt you will have the information available.

There are patterns for 18 different quilts made and a gallery of ideas for inspiration that will also motivate you to come up with your own ideas.

Full size templates are included in the back of the book that you can trace and cut out but I highly recommend that you buy the acrylic templates for the ease of cutting out your blocks. Using the order form in the back of the book or request them from your favorite quilt store.

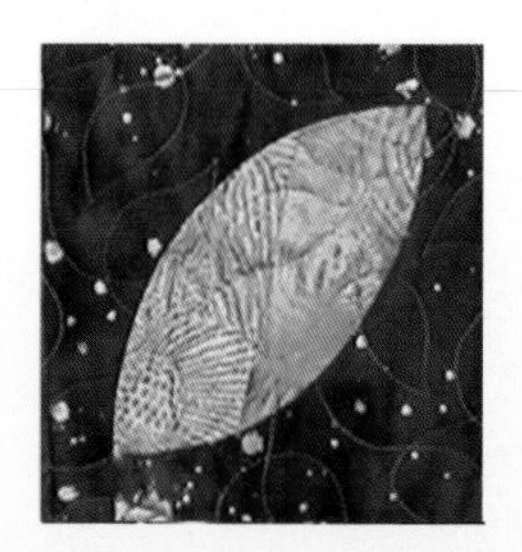

Fabric Choices

I can't stress enough the importance of using high quality fabric. The difference in the quality of the fabric will show up when you are sewing curves. I made one quilt in this book and I used fabric from my stash. I had a hard time making the curves not pucker and even pressing it was more difficult. My machine quilter also complained that it was harder to quilt and every little needle punch showed. In the end the quilt looked nice but if I had it to do again I would have tested the fabric by making a block before committing to an entire quilt made with this fabric. Your local quilt store will have a large variety of quality fabric for your quilting pleasure. You will pay more per yard but it is worth the ease of sewing and your quilt will last longer. I have quilts made from bargain fabric that have faded considerably after only 5 years.

Color

It can be hard to imagine what a quilt will look like using a particular fabric. Take a look at the sample blocks and this will give you an idea of how different color choices work. If you are not sure make a sample block or two before committing to an entire project.

Add some value to your quilt. Don't have your entire fabric a "medium". Make sure to add some dark and light or add a zinger fabric.

Working with a variety of colors in a rainbow assortment can be fun. These will have all of the colors of the rainbow or color wheel in similar shades. When using these I can randomly sew the blocks together and I don't have to worry about what color will go where because I have seen that they will work well together.

Springboard of Ideas or Creative Options

There are so many ways to make this block and I get excited just coming up with new fabric combinations.

Basic Block

Basic block uses only the three pieces of the block. No additional pieces are added. By using different fabric choices you can add a lot of variety to this block.

Let the fabric do the work

Blocks 4 and 5 use the same striped fabric. Each is cut in a different direction. Note the difference the choice of background can make. Imagine these blocks used in a child's quilt as space ships or Easter eggs.

Block 6 is actually four blocks sewn together. A wavy stripe fabric was used on the two outer pieces of the block. Colorful centers were used and a black sashing to set off the bright colors.

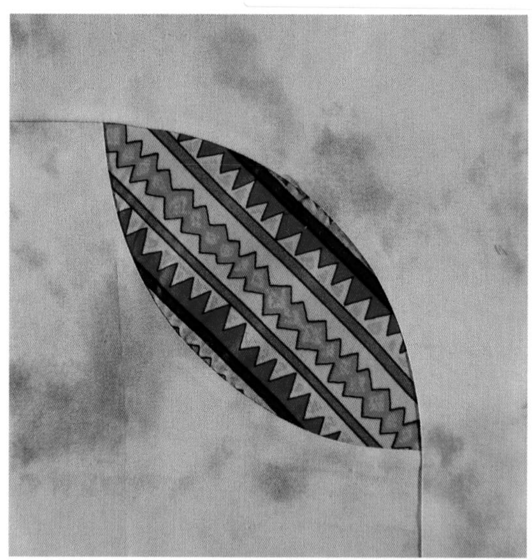

Block 4

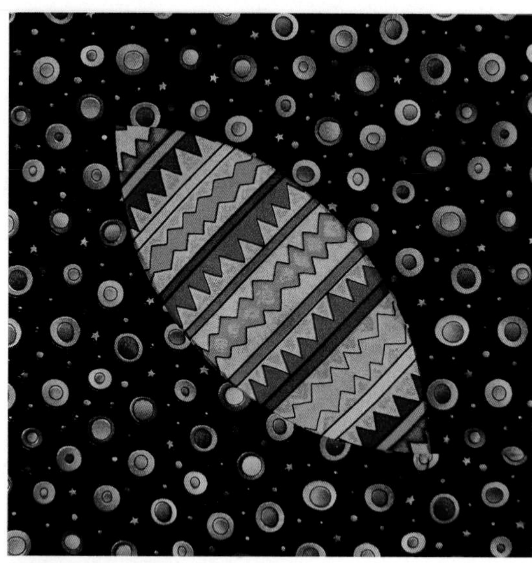

Block 5

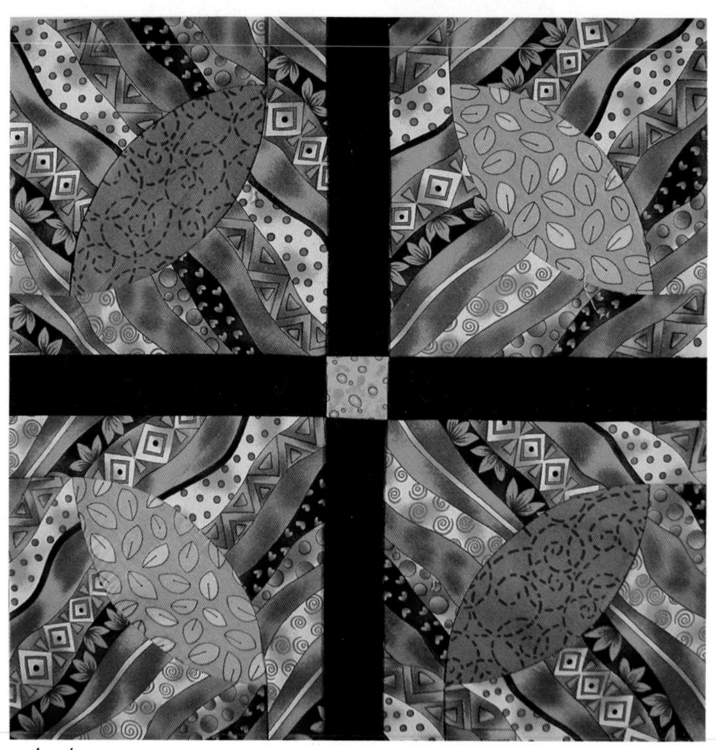

Block 6

Adding A Corner Triangle

Adding corner pieces isn't difficult. You can add one, two, three or four corner pieces. Make them all the same color or add a variety of colors.

Block 7 and 8 have only two corner pieces while block 9 has four corner pieces added.

Block 7

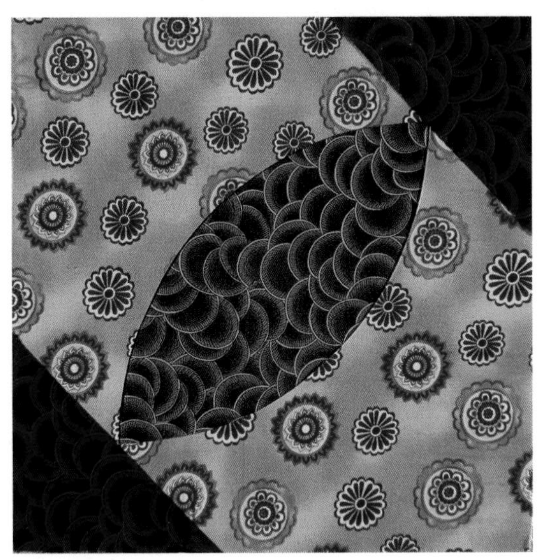

Block 8

Block 9

Center Melon Variation

Sew two strips of fabric together and then cut your melon shape to get blocks that look like this. In blocks 10 and 11 the line goes the length of the Melon shape and in block 12 the line goes the width of the Melon shape. Notice how the fabric choice can make the block look completely different.

Block 10

Block 11

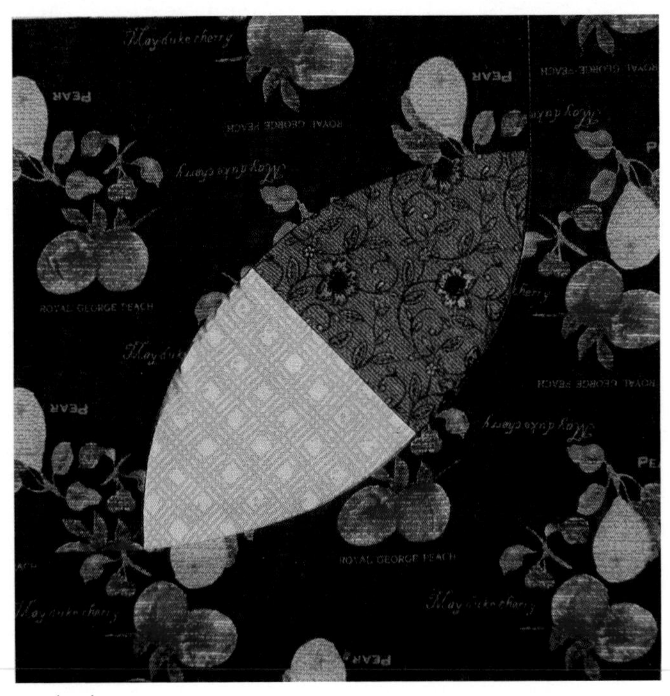

Block 12

Using Two Options Together

In block 13 the center Melon shape is pieced width wise and two corner pieces added and in block 14 the center is pieced lengthwise and two corner pieces are added.

Block 13

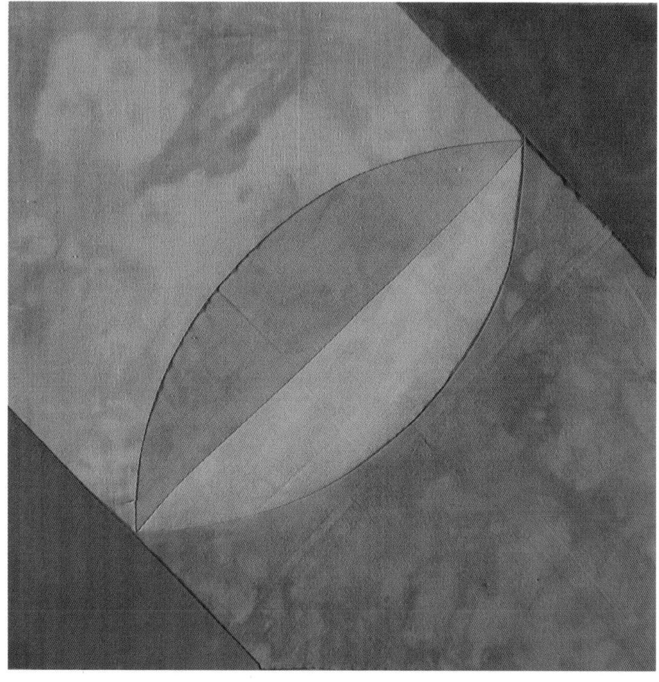

Block 14

Outside Pieces Pieced

Blocks 15, 16 and 17 have the outer shapes pieced from two different fabrics. The two pieces of fabric are sewn together first and then the templates are used to cut the pieces. The center melon shape is cut from only one fabric. Block 15 takes advantage of a striped fabric to add interest to the center Melon shape.

Block 15

Block 16

Block 17

Block 18

Fussy Cutting the Center

Block 18 is made the same as on the previous page but the center Melon is fussy cut around a rose.

Center and Outside Pieced

Block 19 has the center Melon shape pieced lengthwise and the two outside shapes are pieced from two contrasting fabrics.

Block 19

Three options at once.

Block 20 and 21 have the center Melon shape pieced and the outside shapes pieced. Block 20 has two corner pieces and block 21 has four corner pieced. Block 20 also uses only two colors of fabric.

Block 20

Block 21

Center Melon pieced in both directions

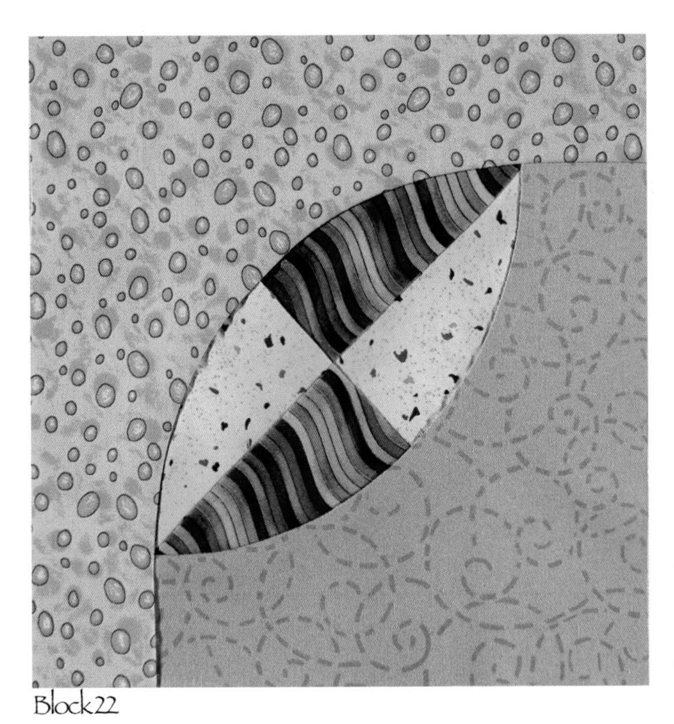

Block22

In block 22 the Melon shape is made by first sewing a four-patch and then using the template to cut out your shape.

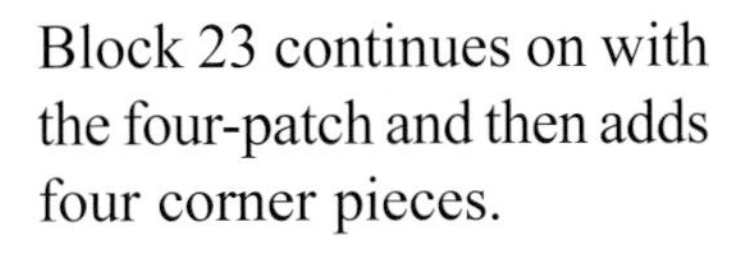

Block 23 continues on with the four-patch and then adds four corner pieces.

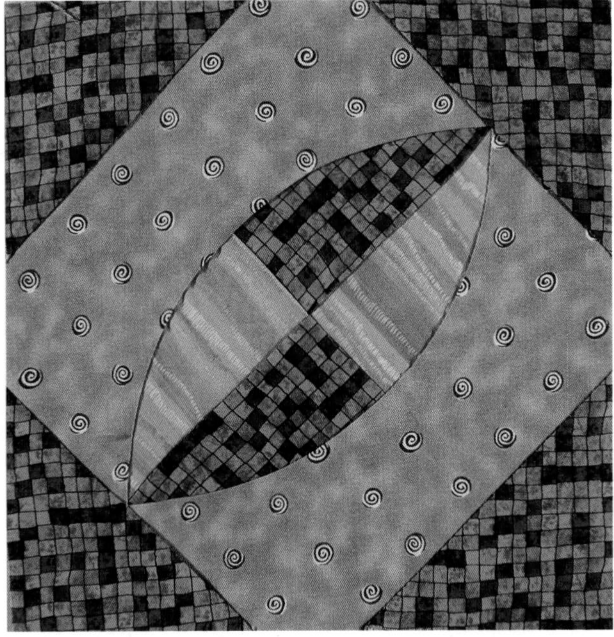

Block23

Block24

Block 24 has the center shape pieced along with the outside shapes.

Adding a square in the corner

This is a traditional looking block that is made by cutting out two of shape A. Then a 2" square is added to each side of one of the shape A. See how the block looks using a variety of different fabric choices. Block 25 is made using batik fabric, block 26 is made from antique reproduction fabrics and block 27 is made from Asian fabric.

Block 25

Block 26

Block 27

Blocks on point

By adding setting triangles on the sides of the block you create a larger block and the Melon shape is now set on point.

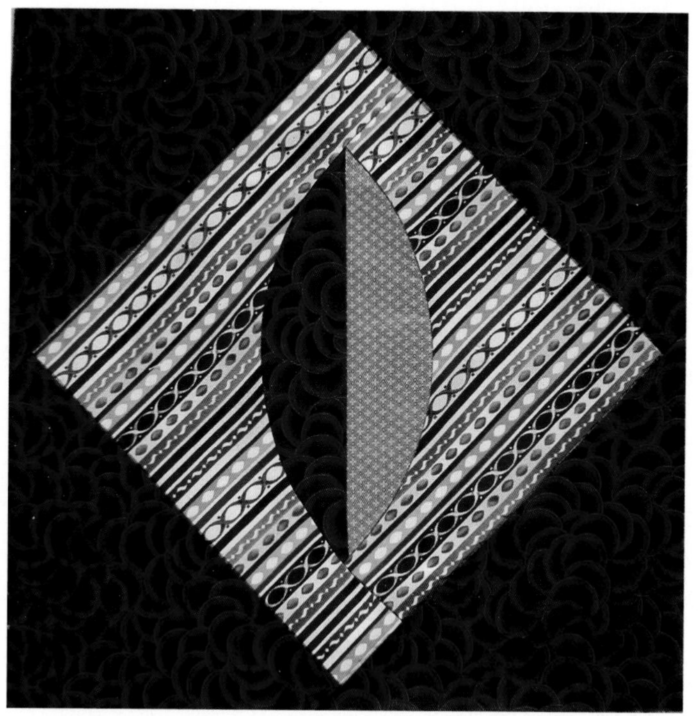

Block 28

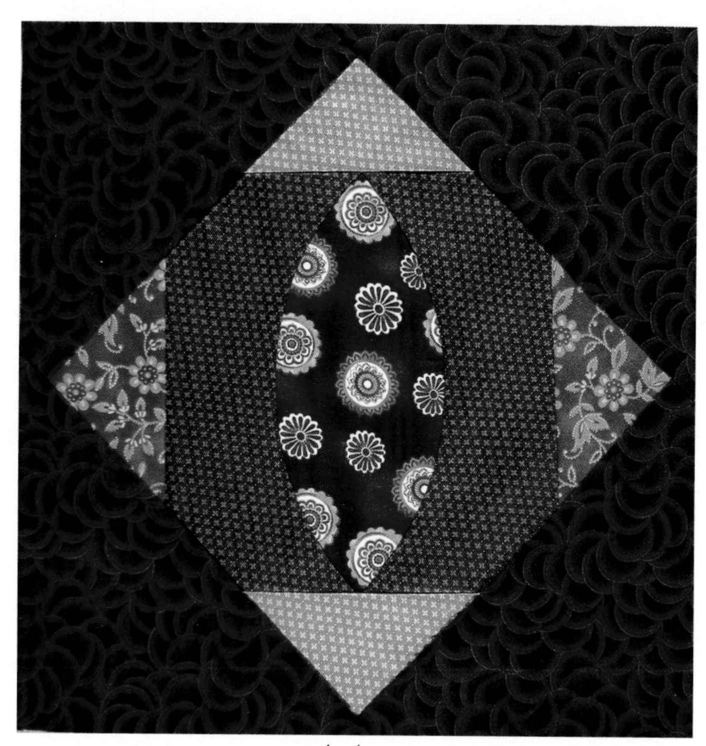

Block 29

Squaring Down the Block

There are times when you will want to square your blocks down to a smaller size to give your quilt a different look. The smallest size that you will want to square down the blocks is 6". This will allow you to have enough room for your seam allowance.
Block 30 has been squared down.

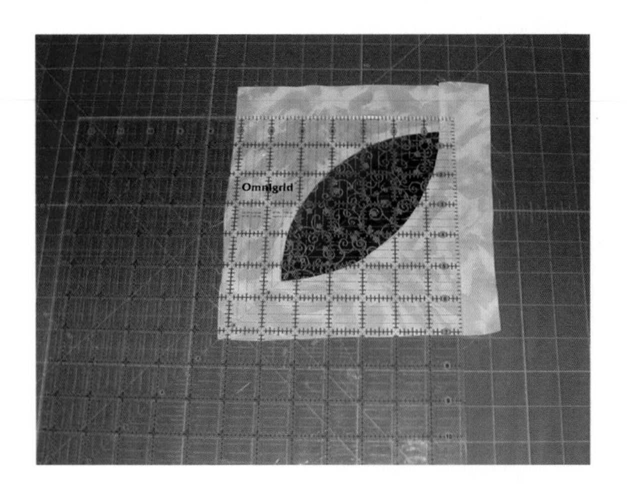

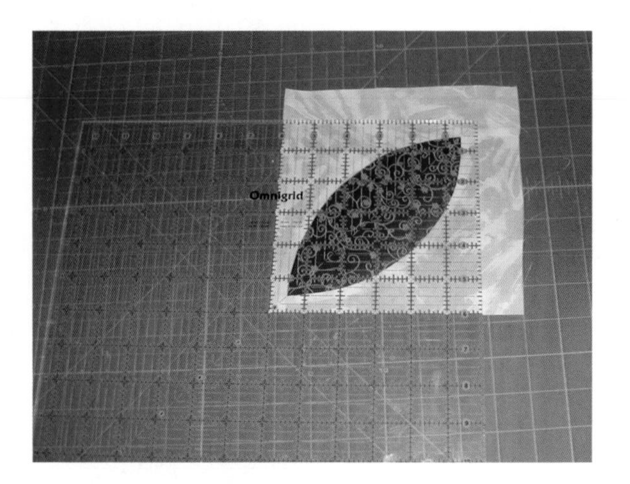

You have many choices when it comes to the layout of your quilt blocks. You can turn then in a variety of ways, add sashing, set blocks on point or add plain blocks in-between the pieced blocks.

Once you have decided upon a particular quilt design it is time to dig in and start cutting.

Step by Step Cutting

Cutting the pieces

Things you will need

- You will need a set of the Melon Block Acrylic Templates
- A 45mm rotary cutter with a new blade
- A large cutting mat
- An additional smaller 11 x 17" cutting mat or a 13" square cutting mat

Tips

I find it helpful if your cutting table is the correct height. An easy way to do this is to use a folding table and cut plastic PVC pipe to insert under the legs to raise the table to the correct position for you.

Buy the 2" PVC pipe at the hardware store and cut it with a hack saw. I would start with about 12" for each leg and then cut them down to the correct height.

The table should be high enough so that your arms are bent at a slightly more than a 45° angle. You don't want your arms straight or the table is too low. If your arms are bent at more than a 45° angle then the table is too high. By having your table at the correct height you will make it easier to hold the templates in place and eliminate slipping.

You can also add some non slip film to the bottom of the templates or leave the paper backing on the templates. The photos in this book are shown with the paper backing still on the templates. This is to make it easier to photograph. You can leave the paper on your templates or remove it.

Cut yardage into smaller sections to work with. Do this by laying out your template pieces to see the width you will need and cut a piece this large.

Because you will need to cut around all sides of your template it is easier if you use a smaller cutting mat on top of a larger cutting mat. This allows you to turn the mat with the templates to the angle that is easiest for you to cut. Place your fabric on the smaller mat and cut one side of the templates and then turn the entire cutting mat around to cut the other side of the templates.

If you don't have a smaller cutting mat then you can work at the end of the table and move from one side to the other.

Or you can learn to cut with both hands like I do. I cut with both hands and this saves a lot of time but not everybody wants to learn how to do this.

Layer up to 4 layers of fabric. Don't go too thick or you will lose accuracy.

When sewing use a ¼" seam allowance unless otherwise suggested.

Lets get to it!

Cutting both the A and C shape from one color of fabric

Cut a piece of fabric that is 10" wide by width of fabric (WOF). Lay out your templates as shown.

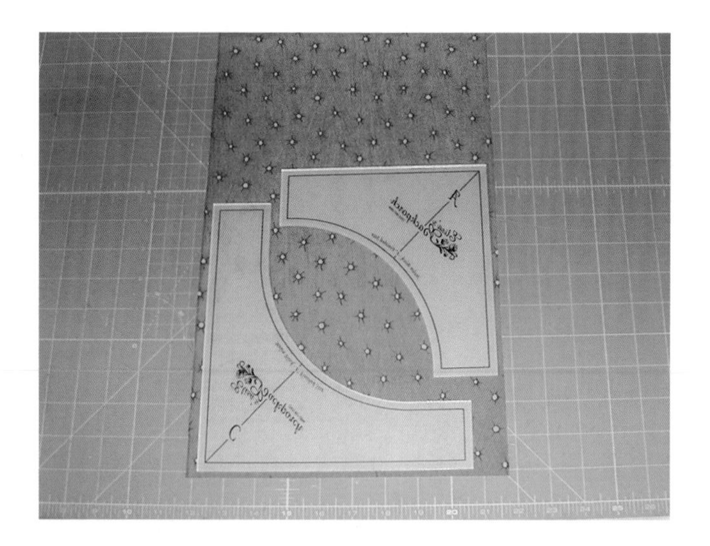

Cut Shape C along the curved edge first. Slide the remaining section of fabric away. Cut the rest of the templates that can be cut on this side.

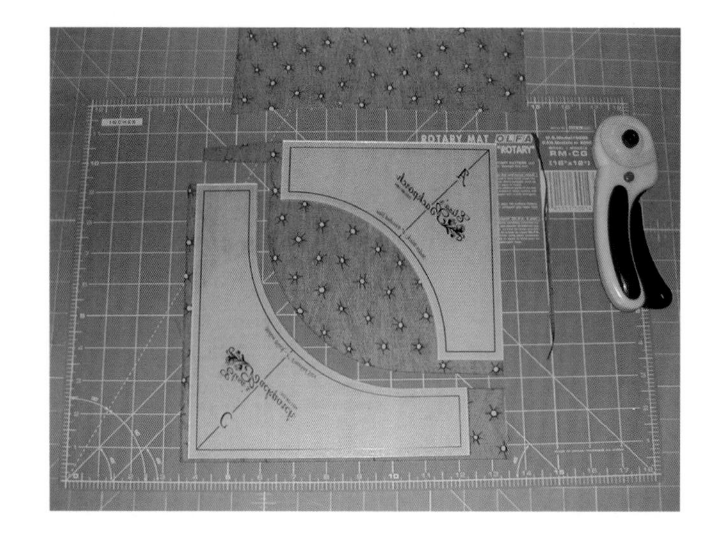

Turn the mat around. Cut the remaining sides of the templates.

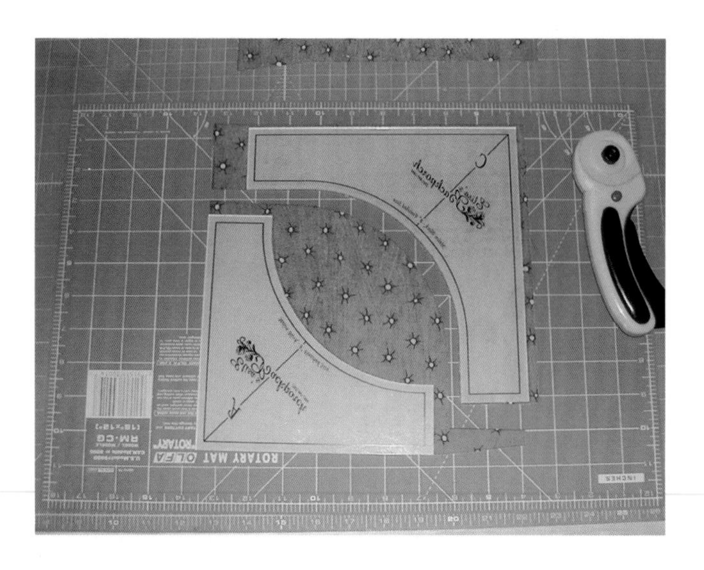

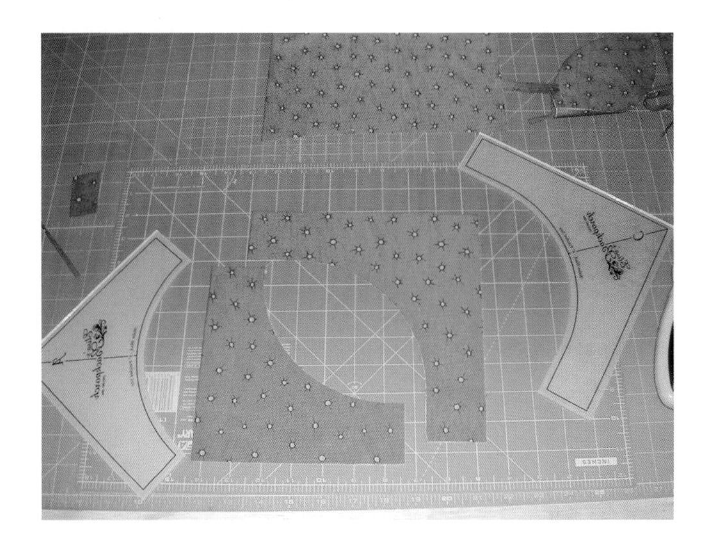

Repeat with the remaining section of fabric.

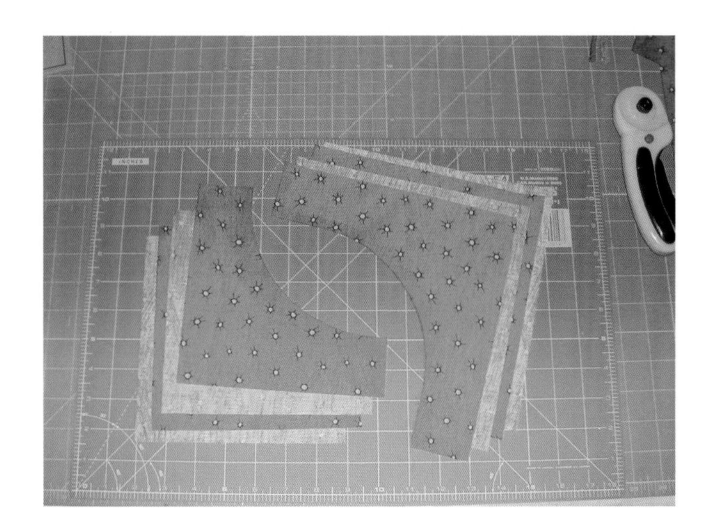

You will get 4 of each A and C shape from each 10" x WOF.

Cutting Shape B

To cut melon shape B first cut a 4" strip. Fold fabric strip so that you have four layers. Place fabric and template on a smaller cutting mat and cut the right side of the template.

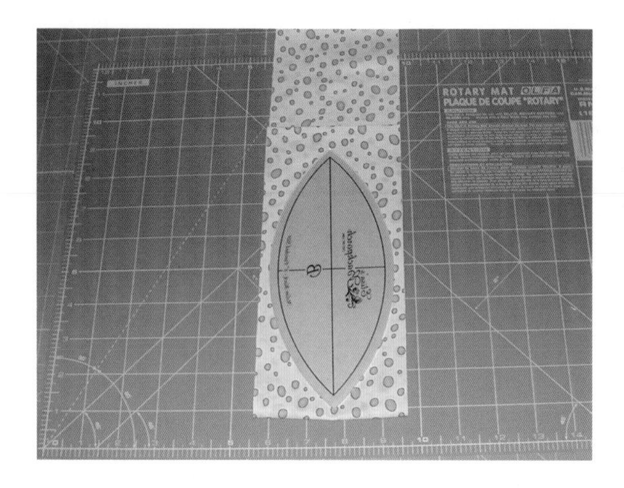

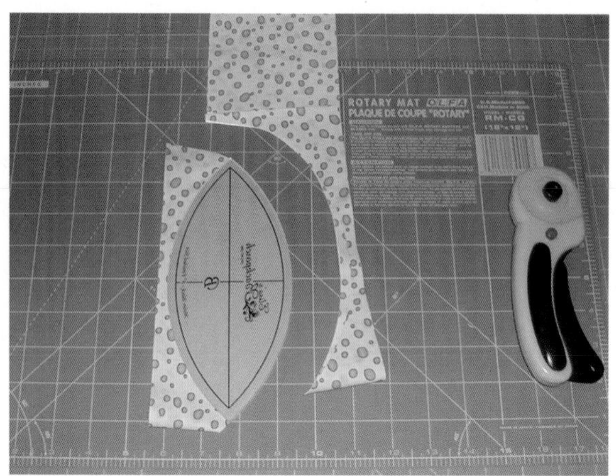

Turn the mat and cut the other side of the template. You will get at least four of shape B from each 4" strip of fabric.

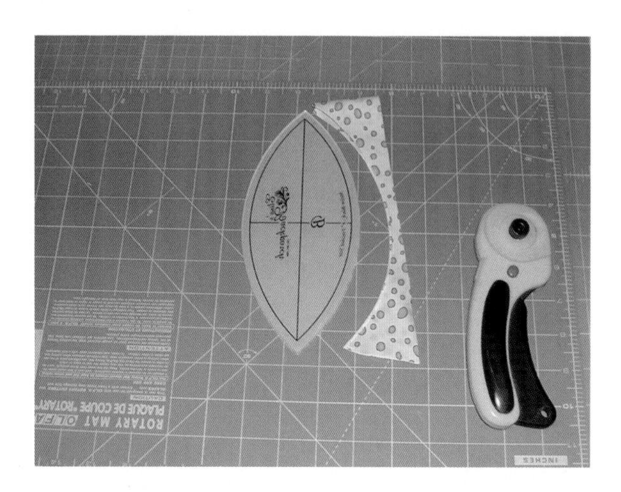

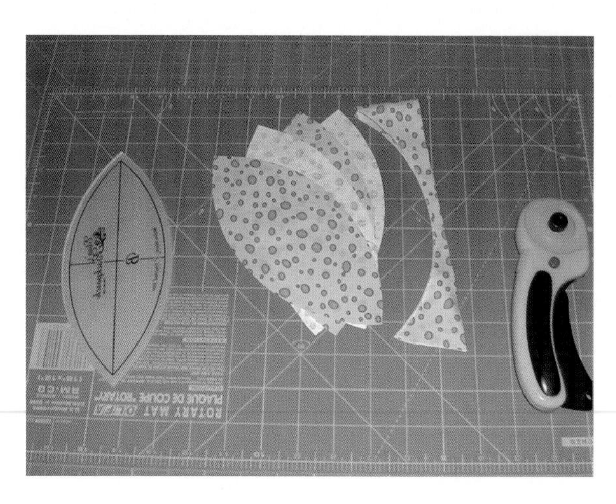

Cutting Shape A with Two Fabrics

To make shape A from two different colors you will need to cut a strip of fabric 5 ½" wide by WOF from each color. Sew the fabrics together and press seam to one side. Place your template with the center line aligned along the seam line of the fabric. Place on your smaller cutting mat.

Cut the curved side and the two smaller edges.
Move the excess fabric away.

Turn the mat around to cut the other side of the template.

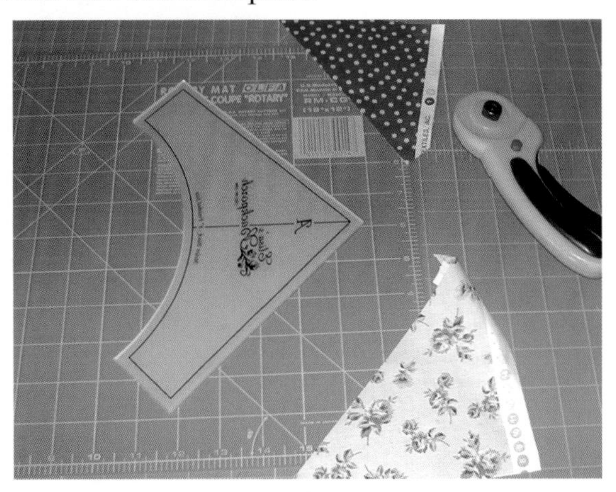

Continue this process by placing the template on the next section of fabric. Cut only one at a time. You will get 8 of shape A from each 40" of fabric.

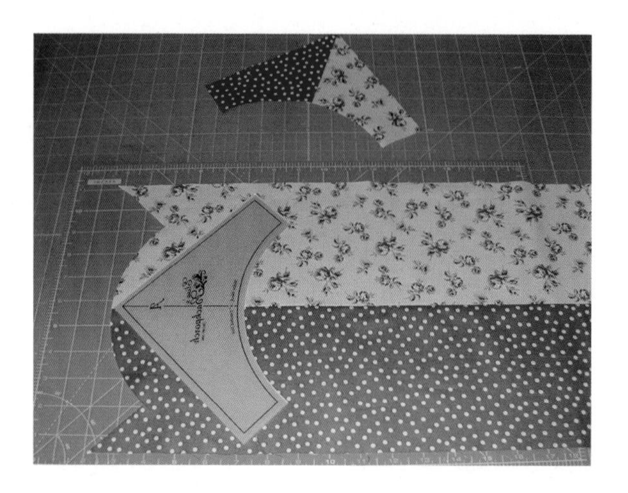

Cutting Shape C with Two Fabrics

To make shape C from two different colors you will need to cut a strip of fabric 6 ½" wide by WOF from each color. Sew the fabrics together and press seam to one side.

Place your template with the center line aligned along the seam line of the fabric. Make sure to check the placement of the fabric so that you have the correct color on top or bottom. Place on your smaller cutting mat.

Cut the curved side and the two smaller edges. Move excess fabric away.

Turn the mat around to cut the other side of the template. You will get 8 of shape C from each 40" of fabric.

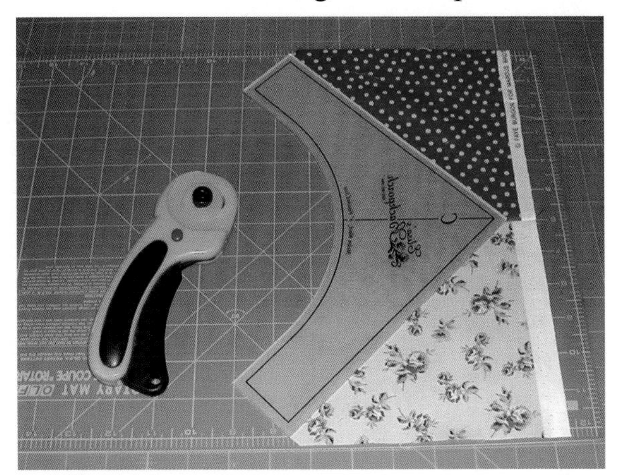

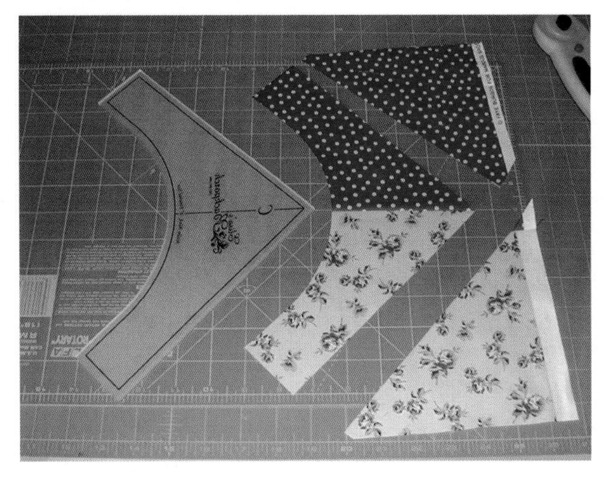

Melon Shape with Two Colors

Lengthwise

To make Melon shape B from two different colors going the length of shape B you will need to cut a strip of fabric 2 ½" wide by WOF from each color. Sew the fabrics together and press seam to one side.

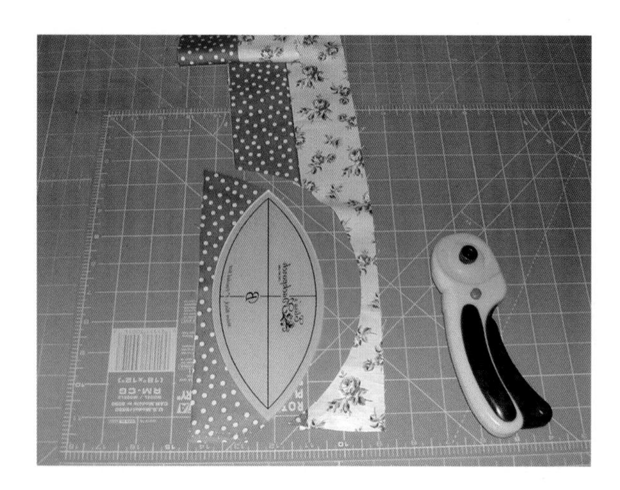

Place your template with the center line aligned along the seam line of the two fabrics. This will be the longer line going the length of the template. Place fabric and template on your smaller cutting mat. Cut one side of the curve. Move excess fabric away.

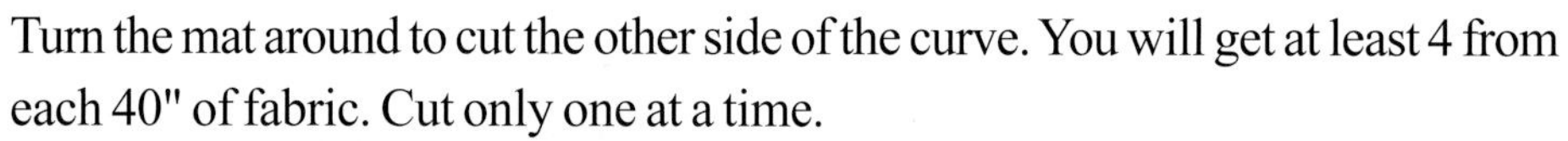

Turn the mat around to cut the other side of the curve. You will get at least 4 from each 40" of fabric. Cut only one at a time.

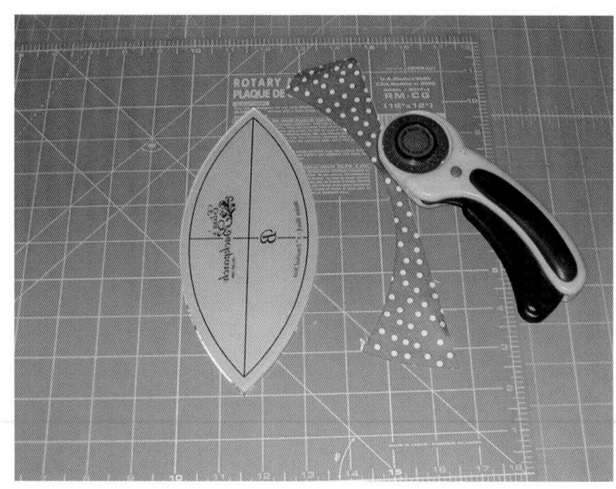

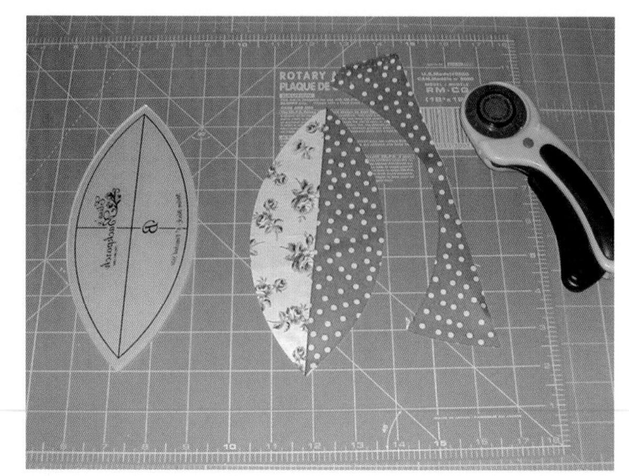

Width

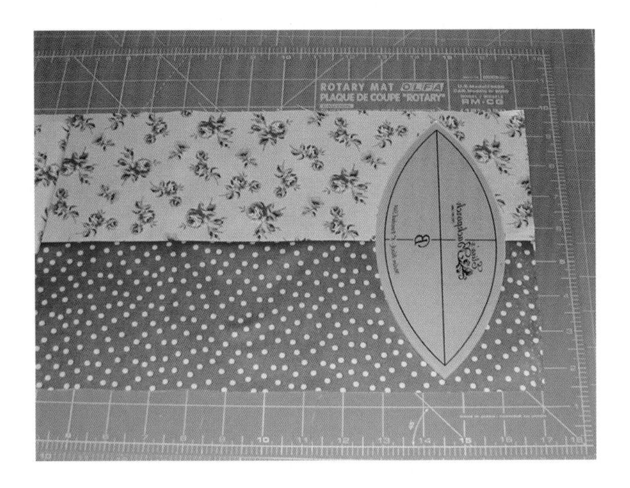

To make melon shape B from two different colors going the width of shape B you will need to cut a strip of fabric 4 ½" wide by WOF from each color. Sew the fabrics together and press seam open or to one side.

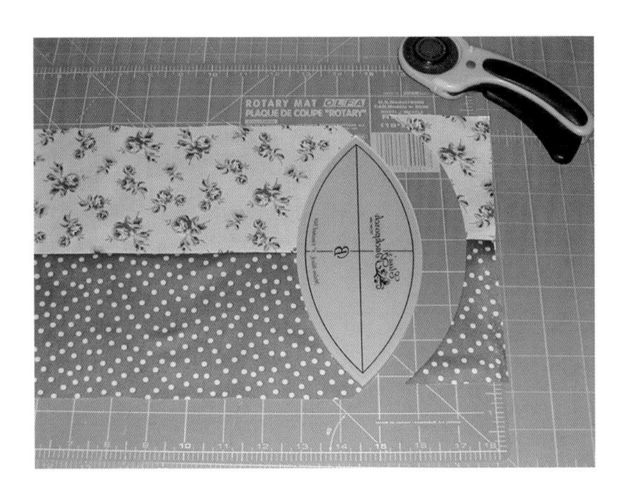

Align your template so that the center line on the template is on the sewn seam of the two fabrics. This will be the shorter line going the width of the template. Place fabric and template on your smaller cutting mat so that you have the point of the template facing you. Cut one side of the curve. Move excess fabric away.

Turn the mat around to cut the other side of the curve.
You will get 11 shapes from each 40" of fabric.

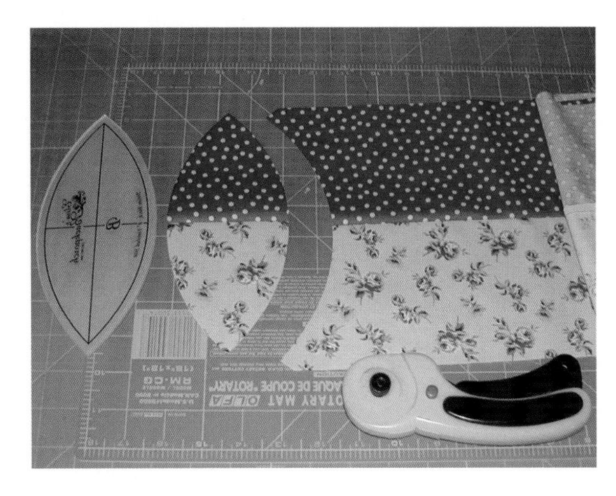

Melon Four-Patch

To make the four-patch first cut two strips of fabric 2 ¼" wide by WOF, one from each color. Sew the fabrics together and press seam to one side. Cut into 4 ½" segments. Sew two of these segments together. Press seam. Cut out shape B as show, aligning the placements lines with the seams on the rectangle.

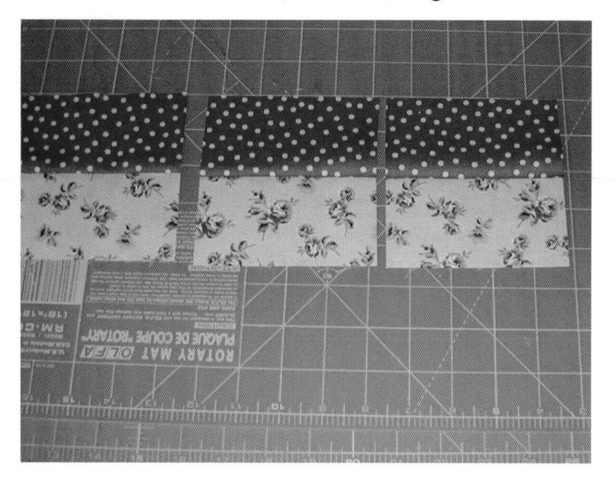

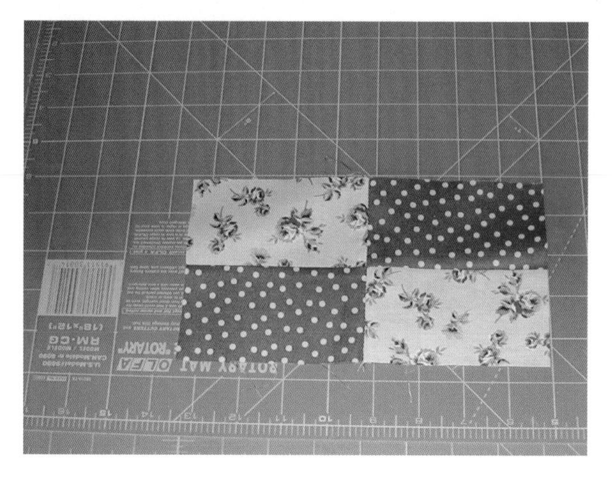

Place this four-patch on your smaller cutting mat and cut one side of the curve. Turn mat to cut the other side.

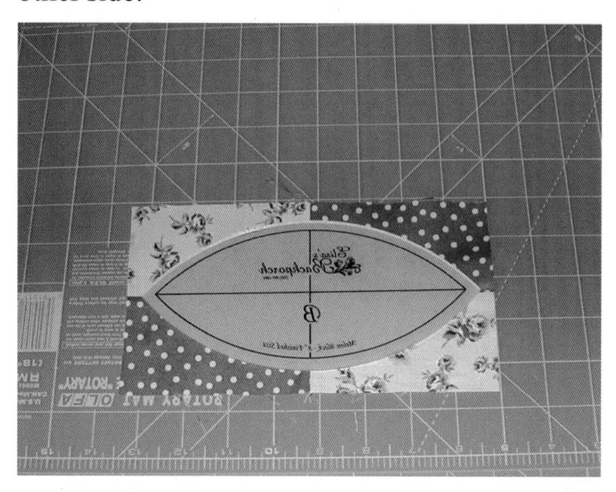

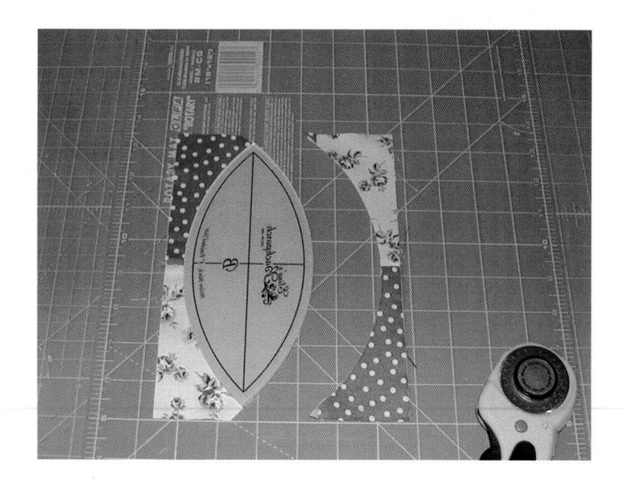

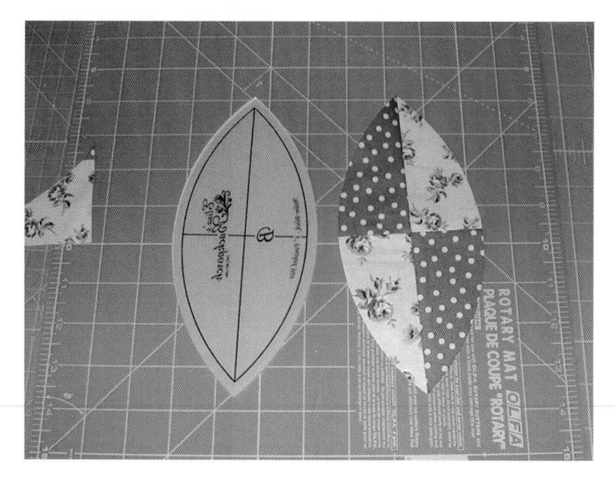

Adding a Corner Piece

For each corner piece you will cut a 3 ½" square. On some of my blocks I found that I needed a scant 3 ½" square piece. Usually about 1/16 smaller. Draw a diagonal line across the square or press the square in half on the diagonal.

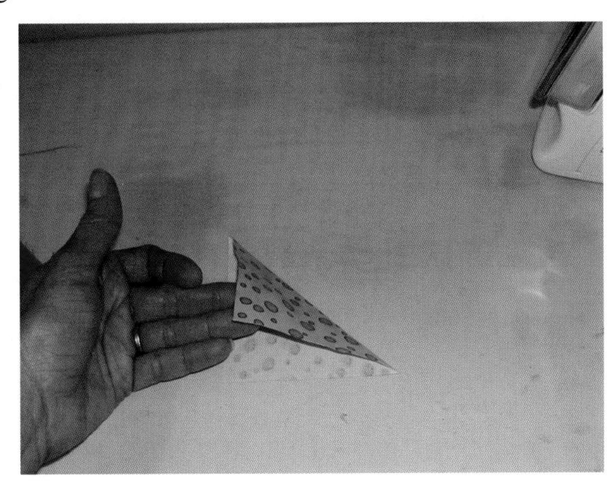

Place this square on the corner of your pieced block with right sides together. Check to see where the fold will be on your block. Open up this square and pin into place.

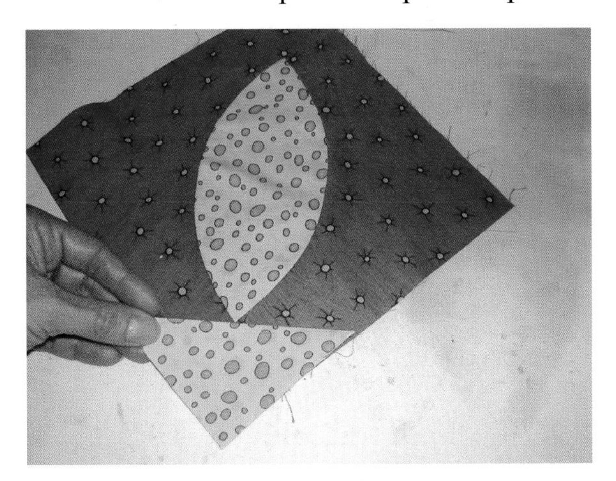

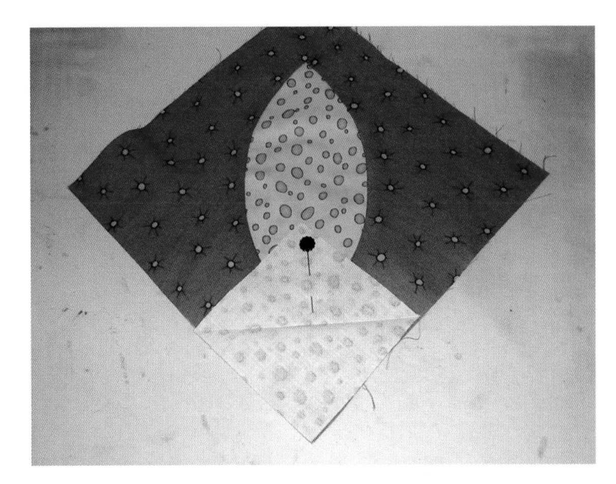

Sew along the diagonal.

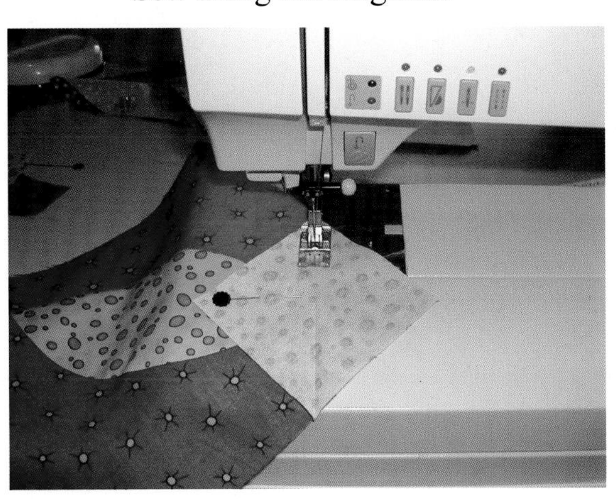

Press the corner over.

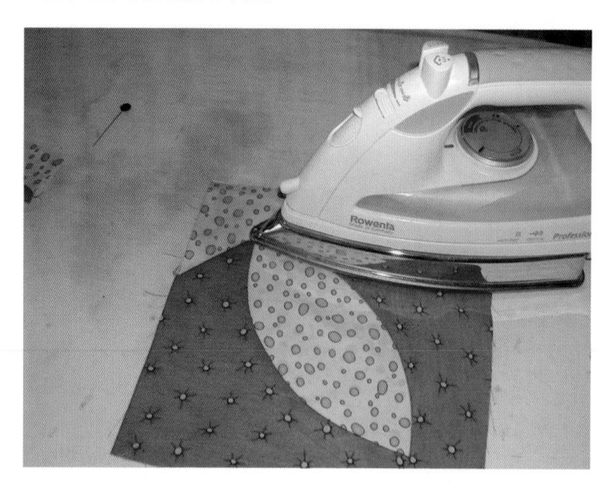

Trim off excess fabric leaving an approximate ¼" seam allowance and press again.

Adding a Corner Square

For each block you will need two of shape A, one shape B and 2- 2" squares.

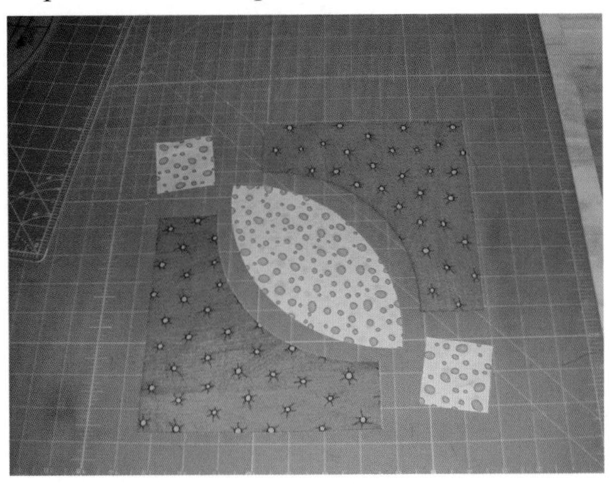

Sew the 2" corner squares on to the ends of one of the A shapes. Press seams in towards shape A.

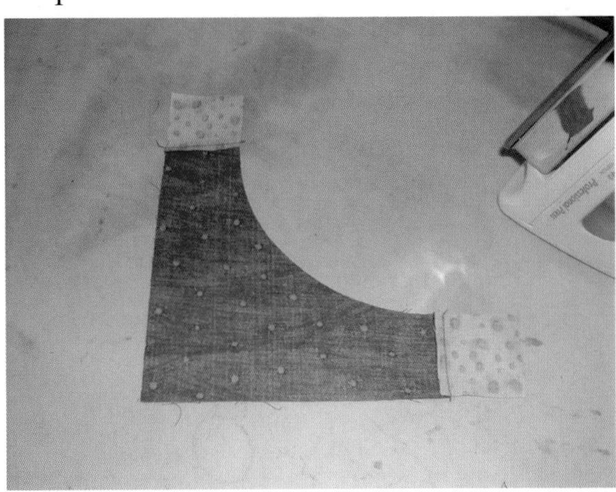

Sew shape B to the remaining shape A. Press seam toward shape A. Place the two sections right sides together as shown and sew together. Refer to "Sewing the Block" (page 34).

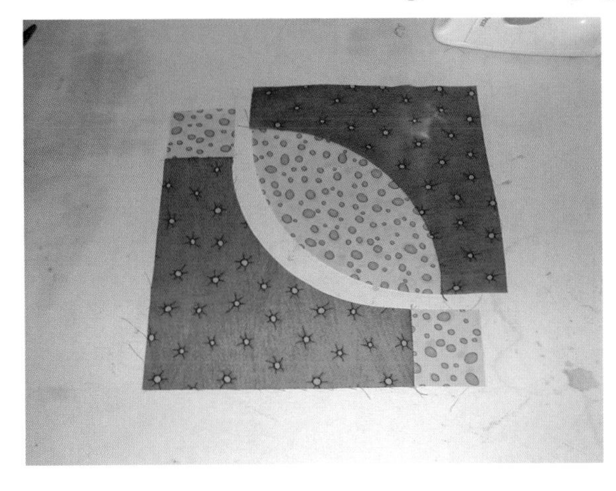

Press seam from the back. Turn block over and press from the front. Seam is pressed away from shape B.

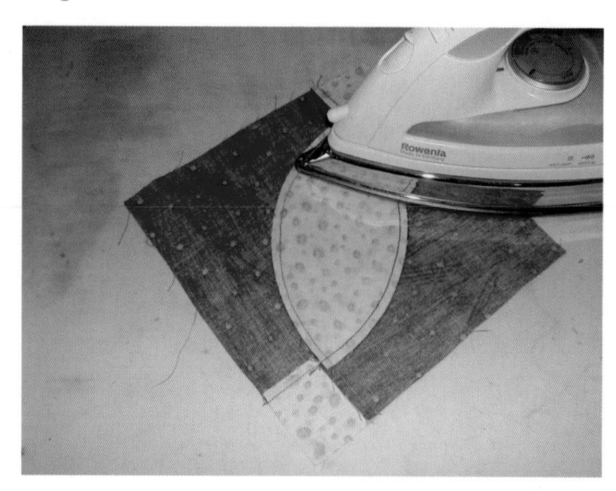

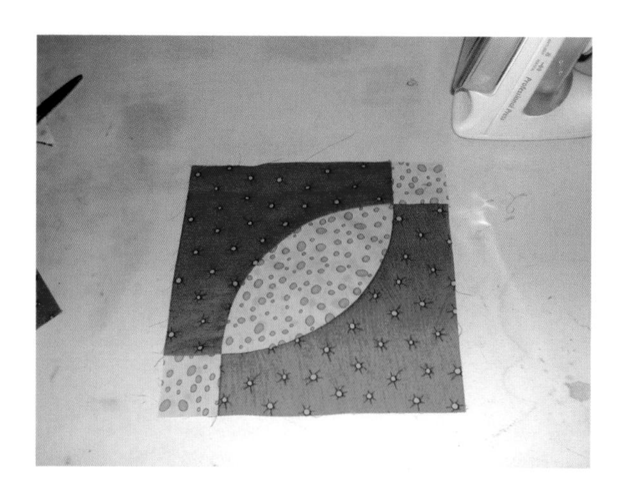

Setting the Block on Point

Adding Setting Triangles

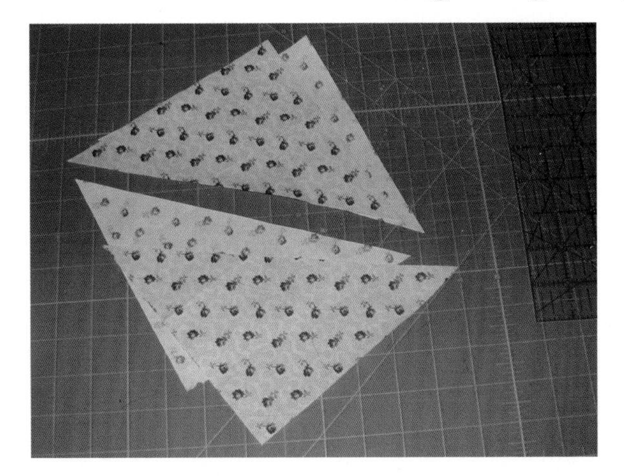

For each block you will need two 7" squares. Cut each in half to make 4 triangles.

Center the long edge of the triangle on the side of the block and sew one on opposite sides of the block. The triangle pieces will be longer than the block. Press seams out. Sew on the remaining two triangles. Press seams out.

The block is now on point. You can trim the extra side pieces from the block at this time. Your block will measure approximately 12 ¼". You will have more than ¼" seam allowance on each side. I prefer this wider seam allowance when sewing the blocks together. It keeps your points crisp when you go to press the blocks.

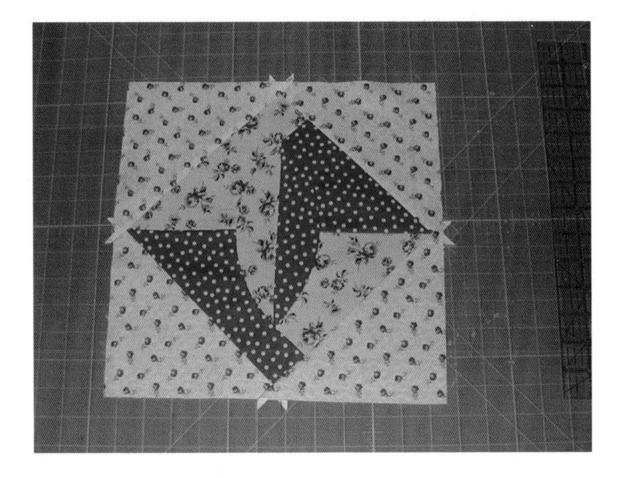

Sewing the Blocks

Curved piecing is not difficult. Follow the step by step directions and you will see how easy it is. If you just can't figure it out then it may be your fabric. I have found that my fabric choice will make a big difference in the ease of sewing.

You will be using a ¼" seam allowance. The seam allowance is built into the templates so if you are not sewing accurately then you will have more difficulty making the pieces fit.

Important tips!

©I find I get better results by using a regular presser foot and moving the needle position over so that I am sewing a ¼" seam. This allows my feed dogs to get a better grip and my sewing is more accurate.

©The L shape will always be on the bottom.

©Use a new, sharp needle. This is especially important when sewing with batik fabric.

Sewing with Pins
Actually sewing with just one pin!

Take shape A and shape B. Fold along the curve to find the center and make a light crease.

Place the fabrics right sides together, shape B on top, lining up the crease marks to match the centers of the curve. Place a pin here.

Align the top edges You can place a pin here if you like. After sewing a few you will find that if you are chain piecing you don't need to pin this section but just hold the pieces together as you place it under the presser foot and begin sewing. Make sure you are using a ¼" seam allowance and take a few stitches. I like to use my needle down position as I sew.

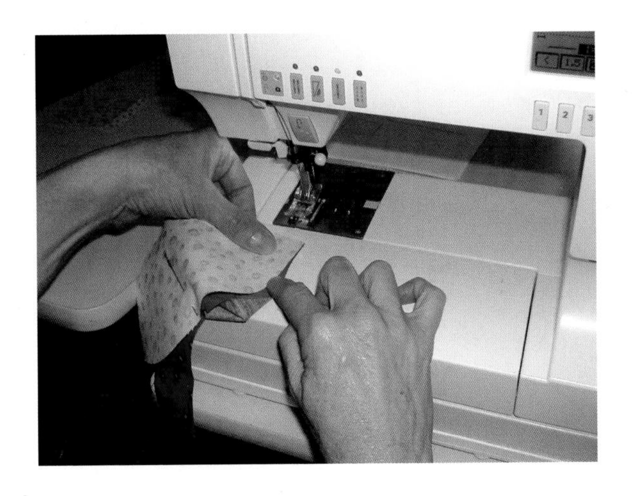

Place your right index finger in-between the two fabrics. Hold the fabric in your left hand at the pinned area using your thumb and index finger. The left hand is gently straightening the fabric as you slowly sew around the curve. Be sure to keep the edge of the fabric aligned with the edge of the presser foot.

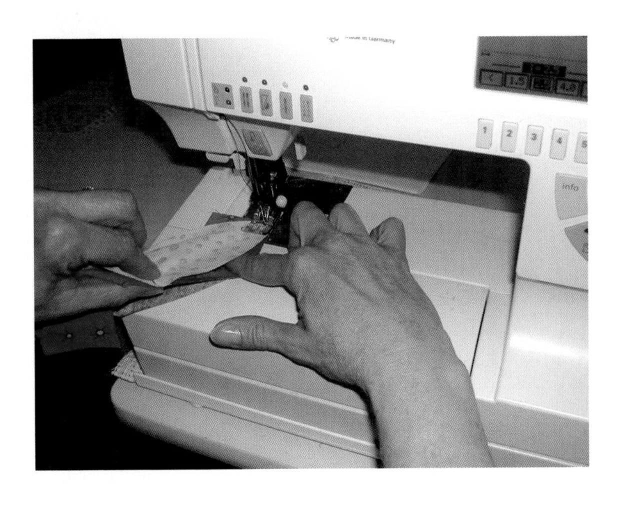

Your index finger on your right hand is guiding the bottom fabric and lifting the top fabric. It is also keeping the bottom fabric aligned with the edge of the presser foot and lets you feel the fabric to make sure there are no bumps or creases.

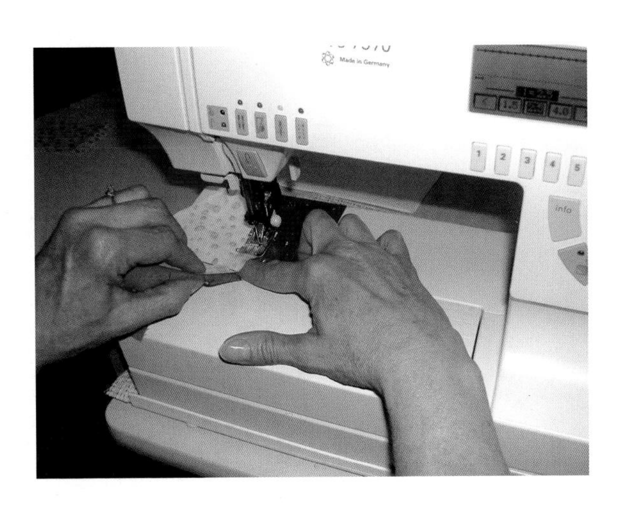

When you are about an inch away from the pin you can remove the index finger and sew to the pin.

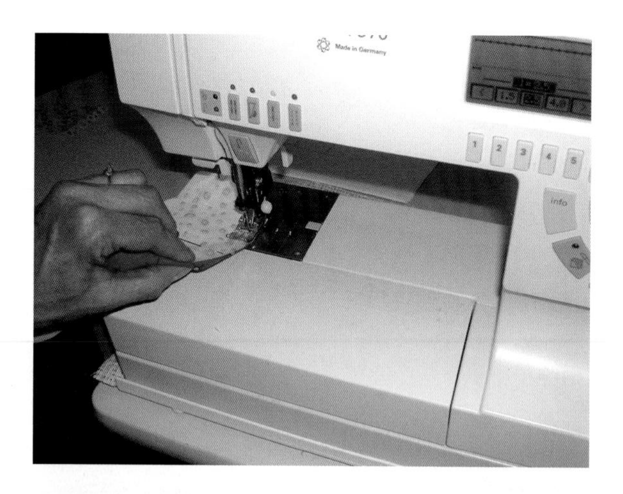

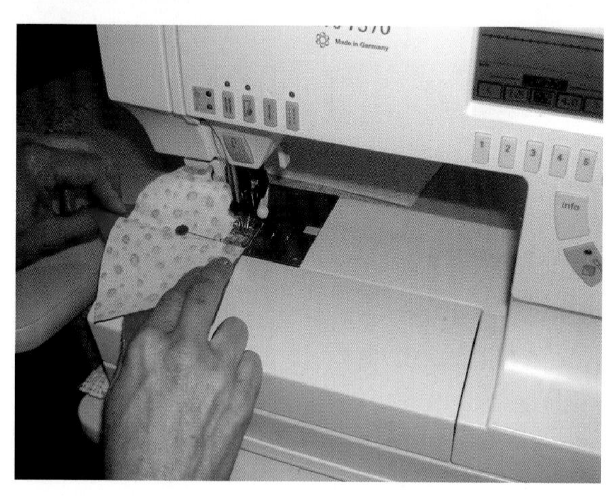

Remove the middle pin. Align the two end pieces and place it at the end of the block. This way I keep moving my pin from section to section. Again place your right index finger in-between the fabrics and hold the fabric with the left hand at the pins. Continue sewing around the curve in the same manner.

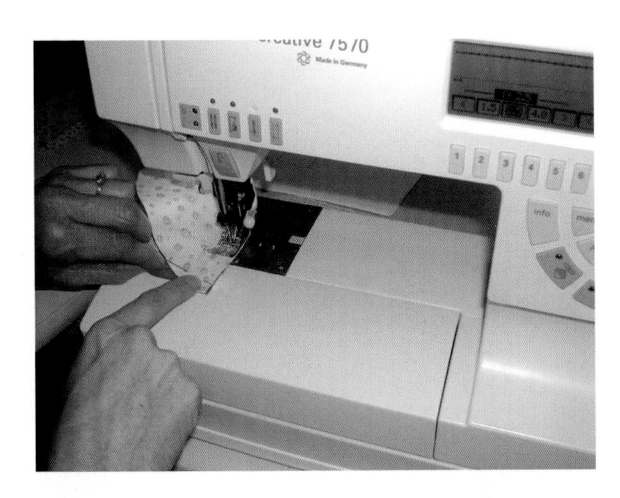

When you are about an inch away from the pin at the end, remove the index finger and sew to the end.

You can chain piece another block into the machine. I prefer to use one pin and move it for each block. You can pin ahead of time but I don't like handling fabric that has all of those pins in it. I'll leave that decision up to you.

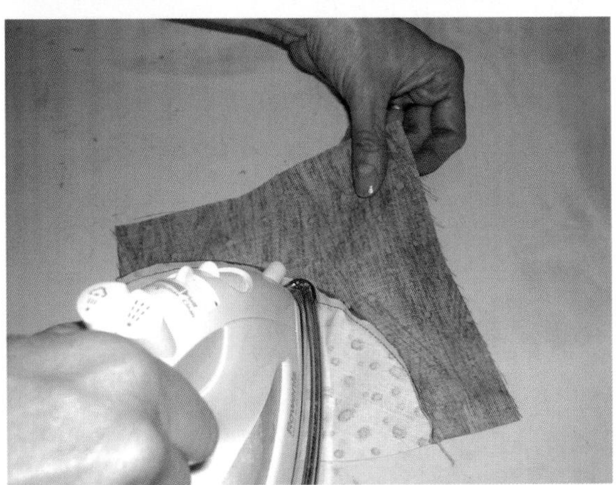

Press the seam allowance from the back. Don't use too much steam, if any.

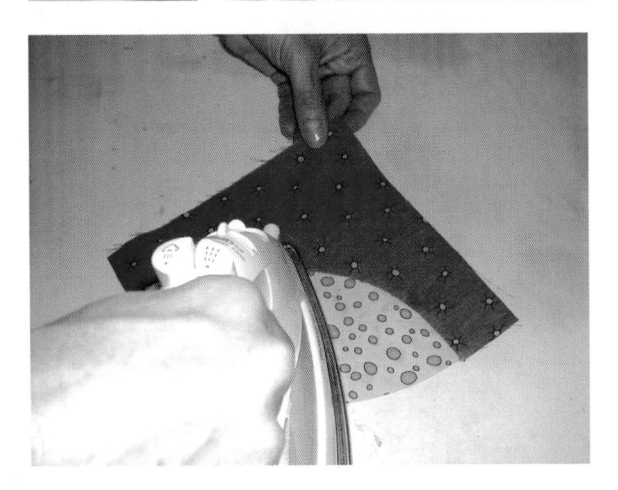

Turn the block over and press from the front. Be careful not to stretch the pieces but be sure that the fabric is pressing at the seam and not folded over.

Now you will add shape C. Fold and crease shape C and your new AB piece to find the centers.

Match up the creases with right sides together and pin.

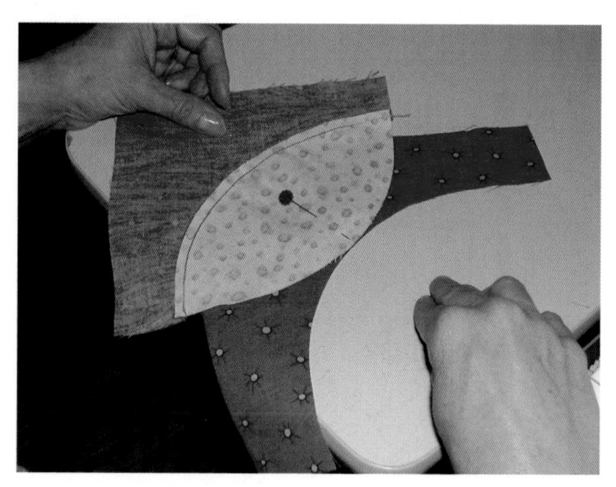

Hold ends together and take a few stitches. Insert right index finger in-between the two fabrics and hold with your left hand at the pin.

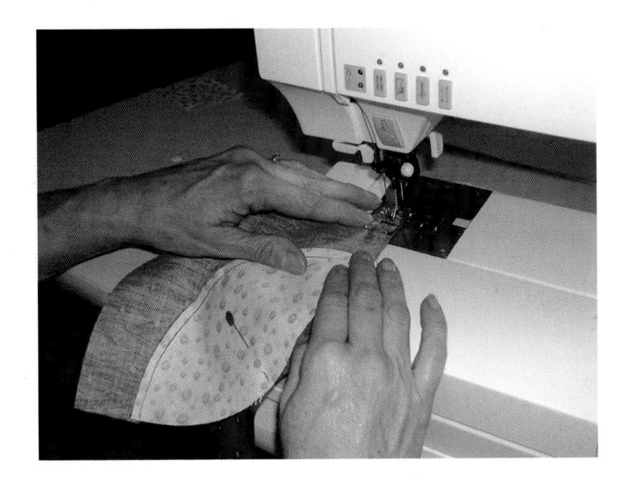

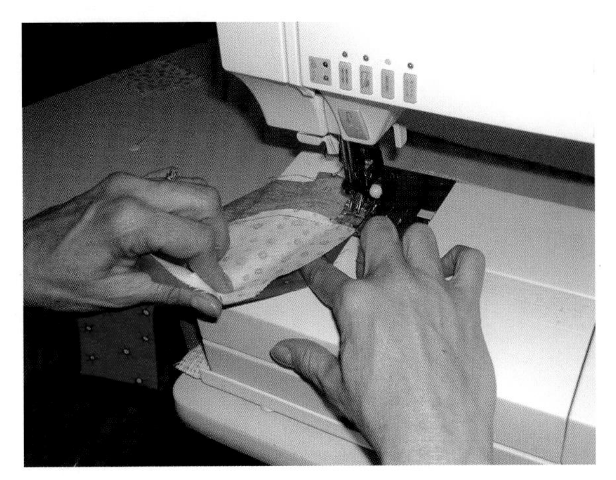

Sew to center pin and remove pin. Match up ends and place a pin at the seam allowance of the AB piece.

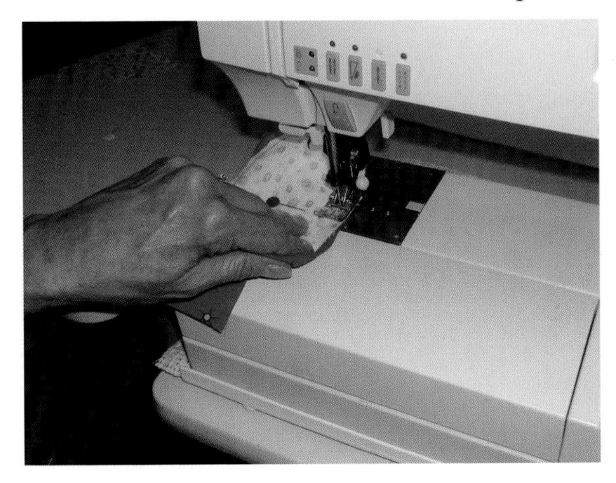

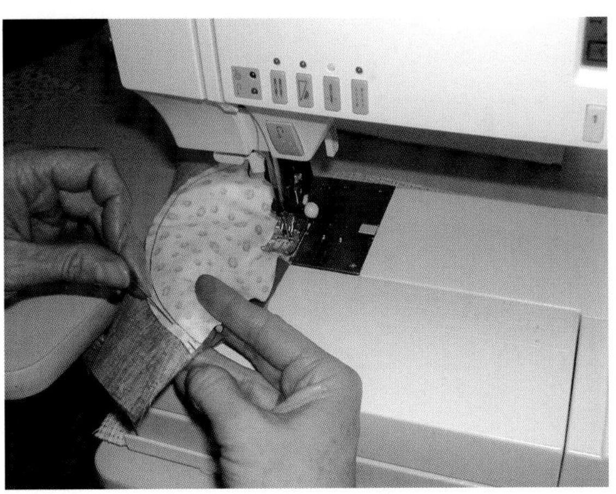

Continue sewing around the curve to the end of the block in the same manner.

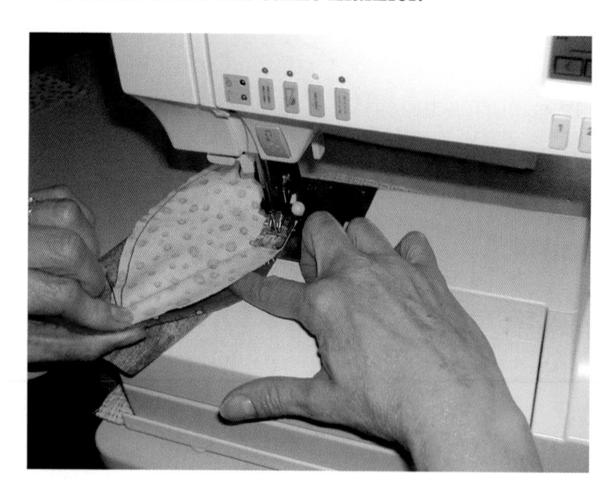

When you get to the pin, remove it and sew to the end.

Press block from the back. Press gently so that you don't stretch the fabric.

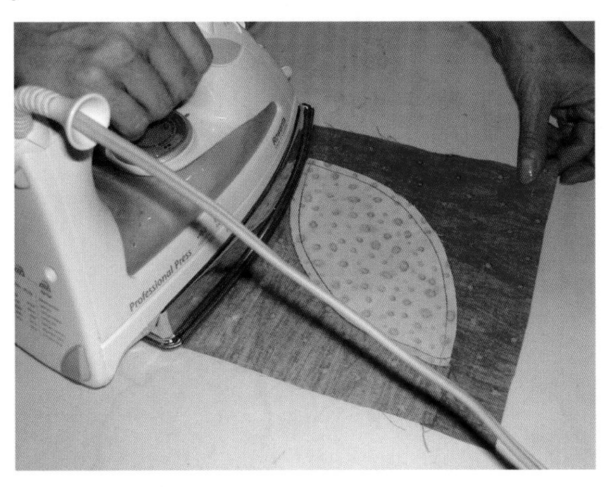

Turn block over and press from the front.

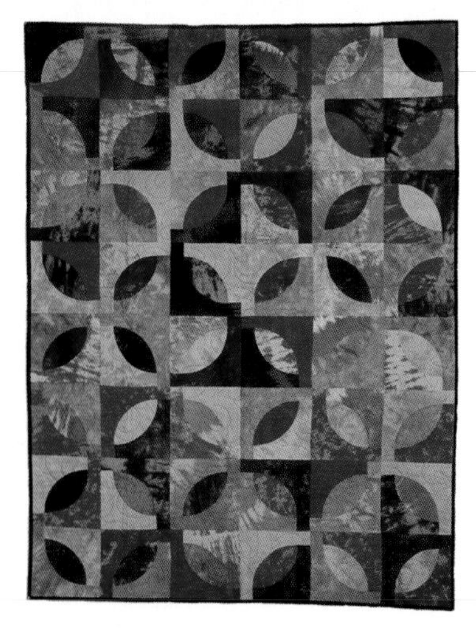

Saturated Color
page 44

Batik Melon Patch
page 46

Flower Patch
page 48

Ocean Swirls
page 50

Fiesta Fun!
page 52

Confetti Poppers
page 54

Lori's Batik Puzzle
page 56

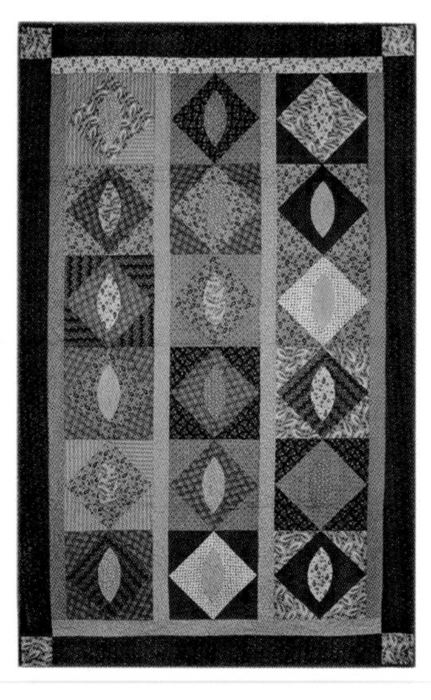

Civil War Remembrance
page 58

Bending Bows
page 60

Harvest Table Runner
page 63

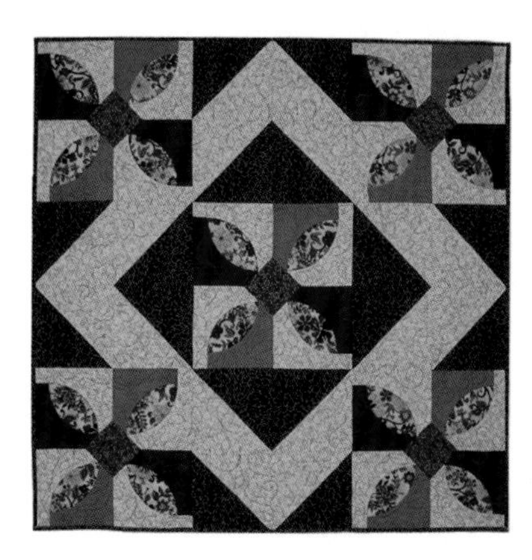

Perennial Path
page 64

Watermelon Wedge
page 66

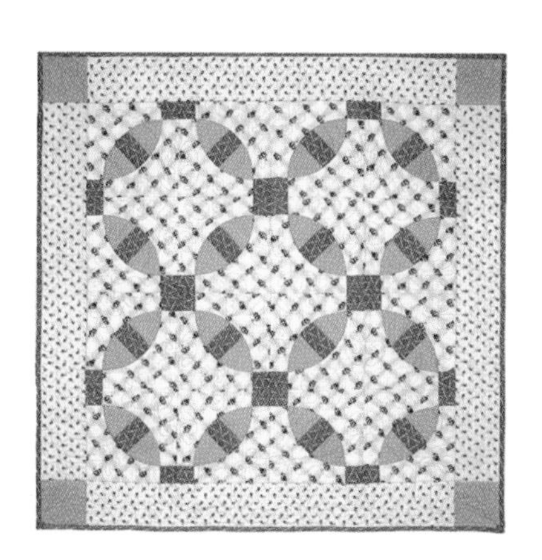

Wedding Bells
page 68

Good & Fruity
page 70

Ebony & Ivory
page 72

Flower Power
page 76

Indian Summer
page 78

The Brakeman's Lantern
page 80

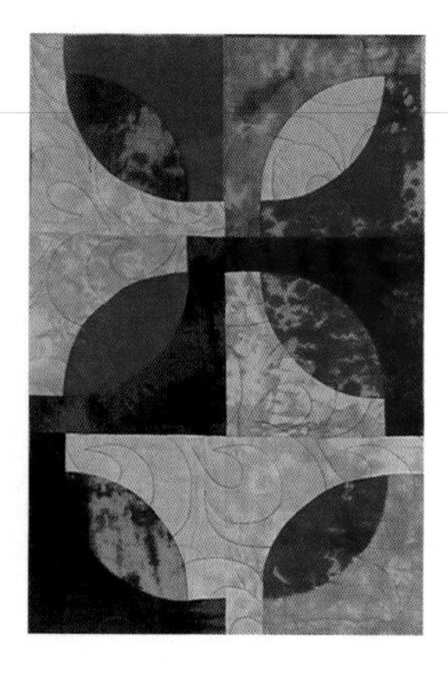

Saturated Color

This block is simple, only three pieces, but by using a variety of colors it looks more complex. The three pieces of the template are used and a fat quarter packet of 20 different hand dyed fabrics. I chose to randomly mix up the colors.

Materials

- 20 fat quarters brightly colored fabric
- Backing – 3 yards
- Binding – ½ yard

Cutting

- 48 of each A, B and C shape.

You will need to cut three of each shape from each fat quarter.
You will have extra.

Sewing the Blocks

1. Sew all of the A and B shapes together.
2. Gently press seam allowance from the back, press seam away from the Melon shape. Turn block over and press from the front.
3. Sew on Piece C.
4. Gently press seam allowance from the back, press seam away from the Melon shape. Turn block over and press from the front.

Assembling the Quilt

Have fun playing with different arrangements.

1. Place blocks in 8 horizontal rows of 6 blocks each.
2. Sew blocks together into rows. Press the seams in opposite directions from row to row.
3. Sew rows together.

Saturated Color

48" x 64" Sewn by Elisa Wilson, machine quilted by Linda Noort.
Fabric is "Color Works, Bright" from Marcus Brothers.

Batik Melon Patch

Only two colors of batik fabric are used in this quilt. Using batik fabric with a lot of color variation can make it look like you used more than one fabric.

Materials

- 4 ½ yards background
- 4 ½ yards for Melon shape and corner squares
- 4 ½ yards backing
- ½ yard binding

Cutting

Background

- 64 of shape A
- 64 of shape C

Melon Fabric

- 64 of shape B
- 12 – 3 ½" strips for corner squares
  Sub-cut 128 -3 ½" squares. Press in half diagonally or draw a line on the back of each.
- 7- 3 ½" strips for border

Sewing the Blocks

1. Sew shape A and B together.
2. Gently press seam allowance from the back, press seam away from the Melon shape. Turn block over and press from the front.
3. Sew on Piece C.
4. Press seam as before.
5. Place a corner square onto two of the corners, right sides together. Sew on the line. Press and trim. Refer to "Adding a Corner Piece" (page 29).

Assembling the Quilt

1. Place blocks in 8 horizontal rows of 8 blocks each.
2. Sew blocks together into rows. Press seams in opposite directions from row to row.
3. Sew rows together.
4. Refer to "Sewing on Borders" (page 83). Measure fit and sew 3 ½" border strips to the quilt.

Batik Melon Patch

70" x 70" Pieced by Amy Varner and machine quilted by Linda Noort.
Fabric is Tonga Batiks from Timeless Treasures.

Flower Patch

Choose bright, bold and almost solid colors for this quilt.

Materials

- ¼ yard each of 9 different fabrics
- 2 ½ yards light fabric
- ½ yard binding
- 3 yards backing

Cutting

- 2 of each shape A, B, and C from EACH color. Total 38.
- 4- 3 ½" squares from each color.Press in half diagonally or draw a line on the back of each 3 ½" square.

Background

- 18 of each shape A, B and C.
- 36- 3 ½" squares. Press in half diagonally or draw a line on the back of each 3 ½" square.

Sewing the Blocks

1. Sew shape A & B together. For each block you will be using one of your 9 fabrics and the light back ground fabric.
2. Gently press seam allowance from the back, press seam away from the Melon shape. Turn block over and press from the front.
3. Sew on Piece C. Press seam out as before.
4. Place a corner square onto two of the corners, right sides together. Sew on the line. Press and trim. Refer to "Adding a Corner Piece" (page 29).
5. Sew these blocks together to make a new 16" block as shown.

Assembling the Quilt

1. You will have one 16" blocks from each color of fabric. Sew these together in 3 rows of 3.
2. Press seams in opposite directions from row to row.
3. Sew rows together.

Flower Patch

48" x 48" Machine pieced by Elisa Wilson and machine quilted by Linda Noort.
Fabric is from Timeless Treasures.

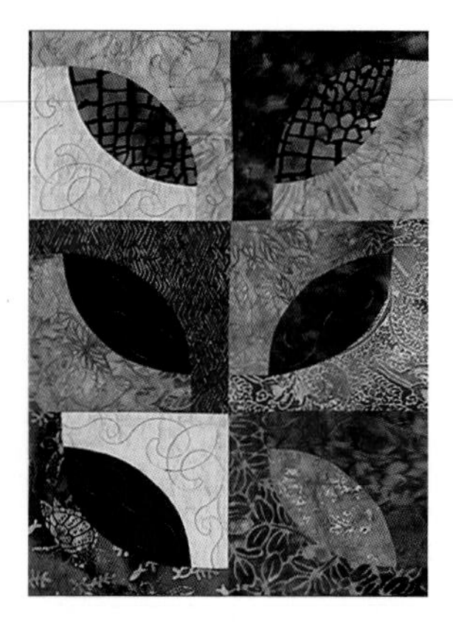

Ocean Swirls

The simplicity of this block allows you to use your scraps and make this quilt totally fun. A variety of batiks were used in blues, purples and greens.

Materials

- Start with 24 fat quarters in an assortment of colors.Your can make it any size you wish by making less blocks or adding more fabric to make it as big as you desire. Batting and backing will be determined by how large you decide to make the quilt top.

Cutting

- For this quilt we cut 48 of each A, B and C shape. You can add more or less blocks as you desire.

Sewing the Blocks

1. Sew all of the A and B shapes together.
2. Gently press seam allowance from the back, press seam away from the Melon shape. Turn block over and press from the front.
3. Sew on Piece C. Press seam out as before.

Assembling the Quilt

1. Arrange blocks as desired. Have fun playing with different arrangements. Turn the blocks in any direction that is pleasing.
2. Sew blocks together to make rows. Press seams in opposite directions from row to row.
3. Sew rows together.

Ocean Swirls

48" x 64" Sewn by Mary Goeller. Machine quilted by Kittrell Strunc.

Fiesta Fun!

This quilt was made by Amy Varner who loves bright colors. She did the basic block and then added four corner pieces. What a bright quilt for her son's room!

Materials

- 2/3 yard each of 4 different colors for Melons and corner squares
- 3 ½ yards background
- 1 ¼ yards border
- 4 yards backing
- 5/8 yard binding

Cutting

Melon Fabric

- 12 of shape B from each color. You will have a total of 48.
- 3-3 ½" strips from each color. Sub-cut 3 ½" squares. You will need 96. Press in half diagonally or draw a line on the back of each.

Background

- 48 of each A and C shape.

Border

- 7 – 5 ½" strips by width of fabric.

Sewing the Blocks

1. Sew all of the A and B shapes together.
2. Gently press seam allowance from the back, press seam away from the Melon shape. Turn block over and press from the front.
3. Sew on Piece C. Press seam out as before.
4. Sew a corner square onto two of the corners, right sides together. Sew on the line. Press and trim. Refer to "Adding a Corner Piece" (page 29).

Assembling the quilt

1. Place blocks in 8 horizontal rows of 6 blocks each.
2. Sew blocks together into rows. Press seams in opposite directions from row to row.
3. Sew rows together.
4. Refer to "Sewing on Borders" (page 83). Measure, fit and sew 5 ½" border strips to the quilt.

Fiesta Fun!

58" x 74" Machine pieced and quilted by Amy Varner.

Confetti Poppers

Materials

- 4 yards Black Background and Border
- 1 yard Copper Melon
- ¼ yard each of 8 different colors; purple, plum, lime, orange, blue, turquoise, pink and red. (or any variety you choose) for corner squares
- ¼ yard paper backed fusible web

Cutting

Background and Border
- 36 of shape A and C
- 6- 8 ½" strips for border

Melon
- 36 of shape B

Colored Fabric
- 144 – 3 ½" squares – 18 from each color. Press in half diagonally or draw a line on the back of each 3 ½" square.

Sewing the Blocks

1. Sew shape Aand B together.
2. Gently press seam allowance from the back, press seam away from the Melon shape. Turn block over and press from the front.
3. Sew on Piece C. Press seam out as before.
4. Sew a corner square onto each of the corners, right sides together. Sew on the line. Press and trim. Choose two different colors for each block. For example sew two purple and two orange on one block. Chose another set of colors for the next block. Refer to "Adding a Corner Piece" (page 29). When cutting off the excess fabric from the corner squares you will need to save some of these colored scraps for the border.

Assembling the Quilt

1. Place blocks in 6 rows of 6.
2. Sew the blocks together into rows. Press the seams in opposite directions from row to row.
3. Refer to "Sewing on Borders" (page 83). Measure, fit and sew 8 ½" border strips to the quilt.

4. Take some of the colored triangle scraps and iron onto fusible web. Trim edges of triangles with scissors to make a variety of sizes of triangles. You will use approximately 60 of these triangles. Peel the paper and arrange in random order around the border. Press into place. You can sew around each shape or just leave in place and machine quilt over each one.

Confetti Poppers

63" x 63" Sewn by Elisa Wilson and quilted by Linda Noort.
Fabric used is Michael Miller's "Fairy Frost".

Lori's Batik Puzzle

Lori was one of the first people to test this template and she made this stunning batik quilt.

Materials

- Dark – 2 ½ yards
- Light – 1 ½ yards
- Medium – 1 yard
- Binding – ½ yard
- Backing – 3 yards

Cutting

Dark

- 6 – 2 ½" strips for C shape.
- 3 – 5 ½" strips for A shape
- 3 – 6 ½" strips for B shape
- 5 – 6 ½" strips for outer border

Light

- 6 – 2 ½" strips for C shape
- 3 – 5 ½" strips for A shape
- 3 – 6 ½" strips for B shape

Medium

- 5 – 3 ½" strips. Sub-cut 48 – 3 ½" squares.
  Press in half diagonally or draw a line on the back of each 3 ½" square.
- 5 – 3" strips for inner border

Sewing the Blocks

1. Sew together 2 ½" strips and press toward the dark fabric. Cut into 48 – 4 ½" segments.
2. Sew two segments together to make a rectangular four-patch. Make 24.
   Cut 24 of shape B from these rectangles.
3. Sew together dark and light 5 ½" strips. Make 3 sets. Press toward the dark. Cut 24 of shape A.
4. Sew together dark and light 6 ½" strips. Press toward the dark. Cut 24 of shape C.
5. Sew all of the A and B shapes together.
6. Gently press seam allowance from the back, press seam away from the Melon shape.
   Turn block over and press form the front.
7. Sew on Piece C and press as before.
8. Sew a corner square onto two of the corners, right sides together. Sew on the line. Press and trim.
   Refer to "Adding a Corner Piece" (page 29).

Assembling the Quilt

1. Place blocks in 6 horizontal rows of 4 blocks each.
2. Sew blocks together into rows. Press the seams in opposite directions from row to row.
3. Sew rows together.
4. Refer to "Sewing on Borders" (page 83). Measure, fit and sew 3" border strips. Press and sew 6 ½" border strips to the quilt.

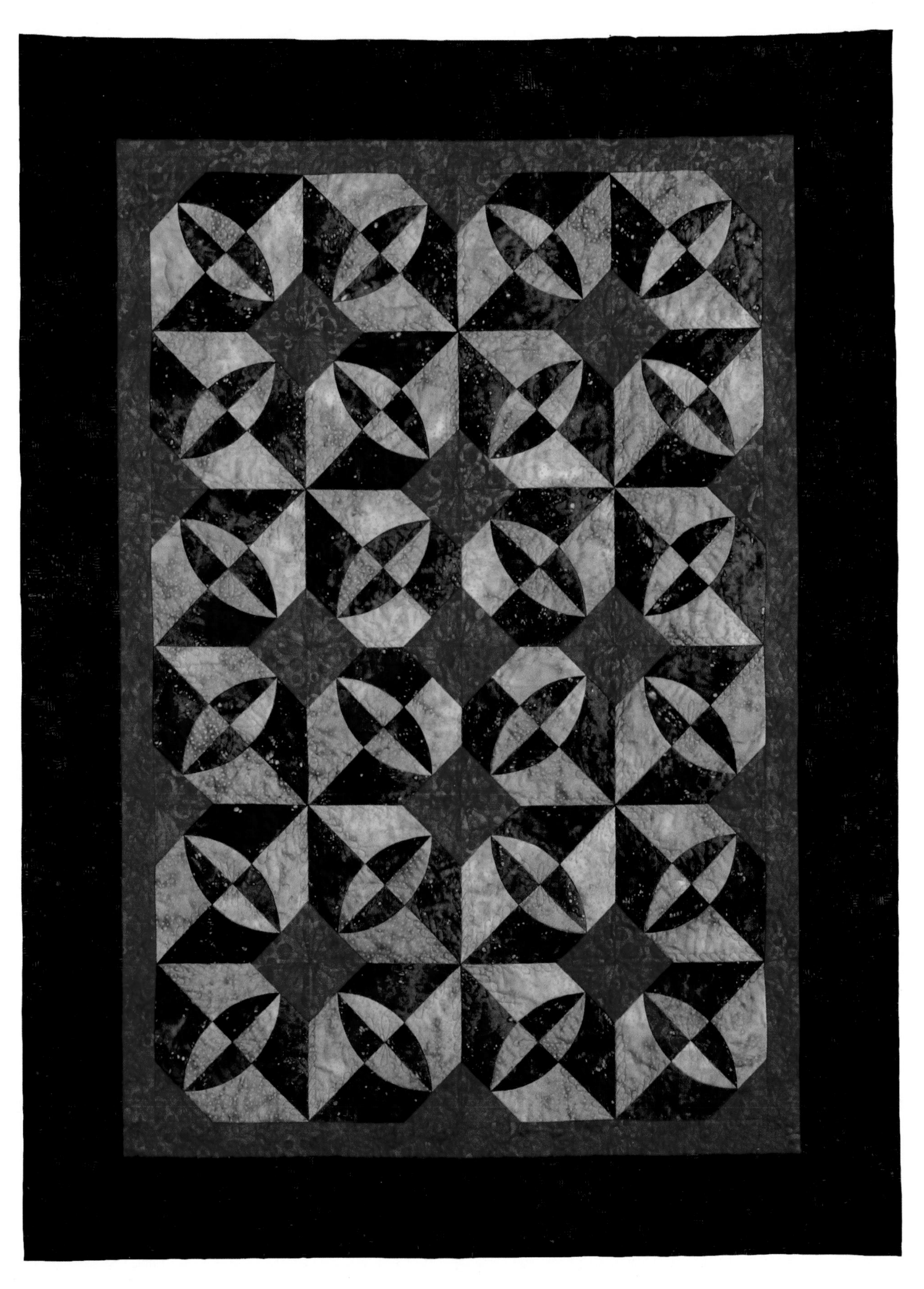

Lori's Batik Puzzle

49" x 65" Machine pieced and quilted by Lori Palino.

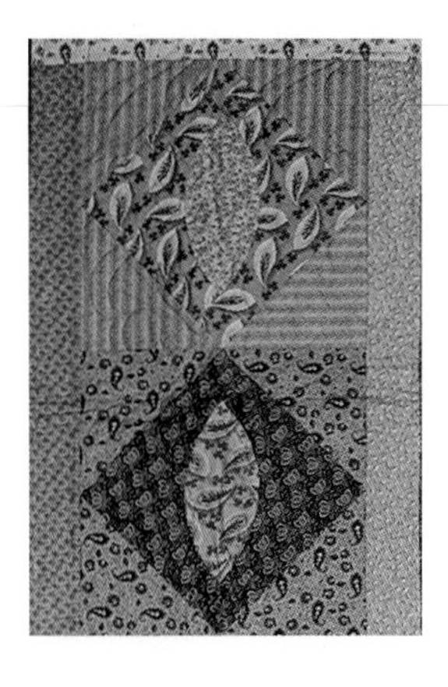

Civil War Remembrance

The fabric used in this quilt was made from reproduction fabric used during the Civil War era. A lot of the quilts made at that time were long and narrow. I decided to add a corner piece to each side of the block which then sets this block on point. Making the blocks into long rows seemed like the next logical step. This quilt has a coordinated scrappy look.

Materials

Use an assortment of fabrics that equal the total yardage if desired.

- 2 yards Pink
- 2 yards Green
- 3 yards Brown
- 5 yards Backing
- 5/8 yard Binding

Cutting

Pinks

- 5 – 4" strips. Sub-cut 18 of shape B
- 10 – 3 ½" strips by WOF

Greens

- 9 of Shape A and C
- 18 – 7" squares; cut each in half on the diagonal for setting triangles
- 4 – 5" squares for outer border

Browns

- 9 of shape A and C
- 18 – 7" squares; cut each in half on the diagonal for setting triangles
- 6 – 5" strips for outer border

Sewing the Blocks

1. Sew all of the A and B shapes together. Press seam allowance from the back, press away from the Melon shape. Turn block over and press from the front.
2. Sew on Piece C. Each block will have the same A and C fabric. If this fabric is green then choose a brown fabric for the setting triangles. If the A – C fabric is brown then choose green setting triangles.
4. Sew on the setting triangles. Refer "Setting the Block on Point" (page 33). You will have 18 blocks that measure approximately 12 ¼". Square up if desired, but leave more than ¼" for seam allowance.

Assembling the Quilt

1. Sew together 6 blocks to make a row. Make 3 vertical rows. These rows will measure approximately 72".
2. Sew pink inner border strips together end to end. Measure and cut 4 strips the length of the rows which will be approximately 72".
3. Sew the pink strips and blocks together in vertical rows. Begin and end with a pink strip.

4. Cut two more pink strips the width of the quilt top. Sew one on the top and bottom of the quilt.
5. Sew outer border strips together. Refer to "Sewing on Borders" (page 83). Measure and cut two strips the width and two strips the length of the quilt top.
6. Pin and sew the two longer strips on to the sides of the top.
7. Sew the Green 5" squares on to the two shorter strips. Pin and sew these on to the top and bottom of the quilt top.

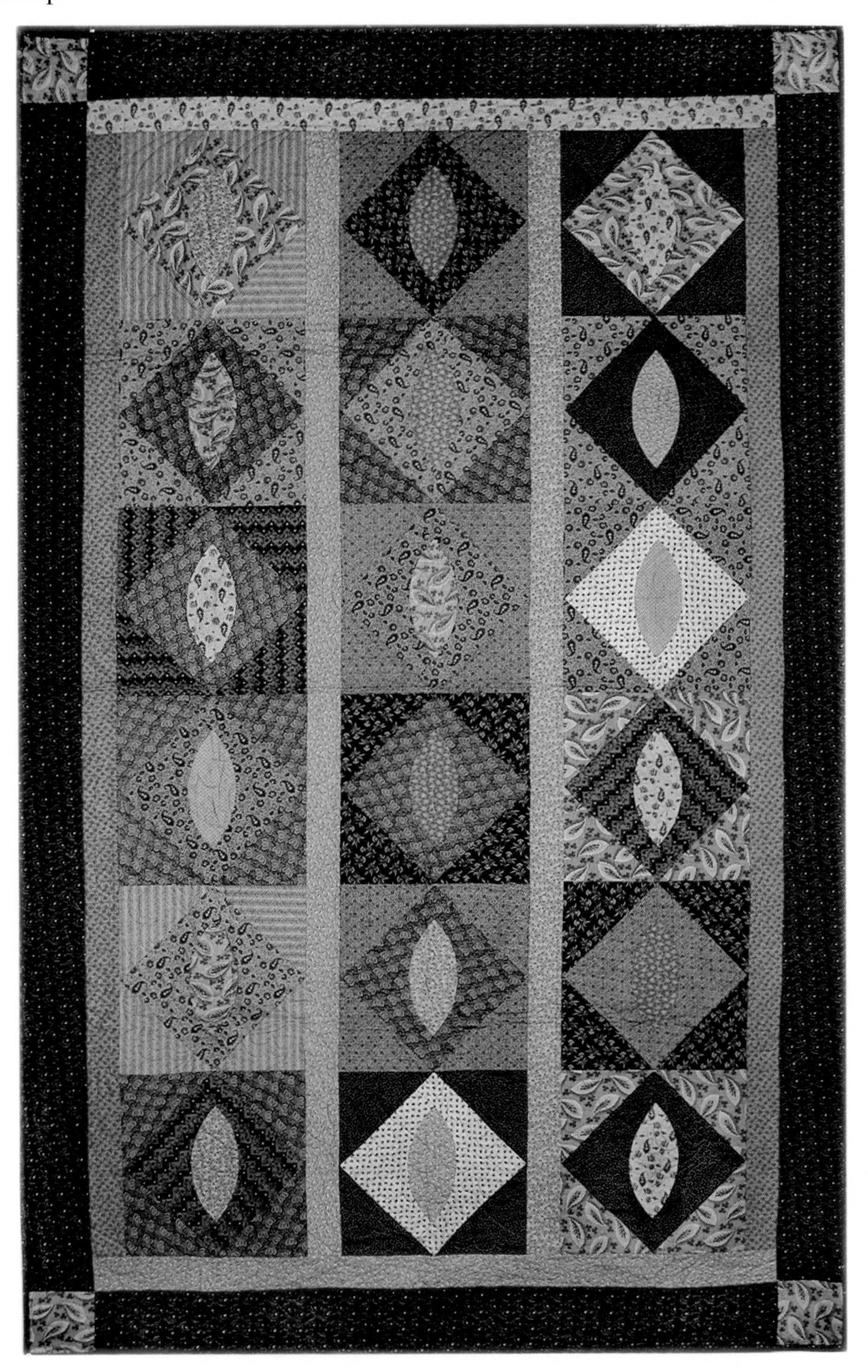

Civil War Remembrance

57" x 87" Sewn by Elisa Wilson, machine quilted by Linda Noort.
Fabric is "Charleston" by Marcus Brothers.

Bending Bows

Only two colors are used in this quilt. The Melon fabric is shown in the picture. By using a fabric with subtle rows like this one you get variety in the completed blocks. Instead of a straight corner piece I chose to make a curved corner piece. While this is just a bit more work I found the result to be worth it.

Materials

- Main color – 4 yards, includes border and binding.
- Background – 2 ¾ yards
- Freezer paper

Cutting

Main fabric

- 36 of shape B
- 9 – 4 ½" strips. Sub-cut 72 – 4 ½" squares
- 5 – 6 ½" strips for border
- 5 – 2 ½" strips for binding

Background

- 36 each of shape A and C.

Freezer paper

- 4 ½" squares

Sewing the Blocks

1. Sew all of the A and B shapes together.
2. Gently press seam allowance from the back, press seam away from the Melon shape. Turn block over and press from the front.
3. Sew on Piece C. Press seam out as before.
4. Trace the curved corner template onto the dull side of a 4 ½" square of freezer paper. You can make a few of these and re-use until they are no longer sticky.

5. Iron freezer paper to the wrong side of the 4 ½" square. Cut away extra fabric leaving approximately ¼" seam. Press over this seam allowance.

6. Press this ¼" to the back of the freezer paper. Add a few drops of glue on the seam allowance and place on the corner of the sewn block. Press to set the glue.

7. Turn this piece of fabric so that you can see the seam. Remove the freezer paper and stitch along this pressed seam line. Press again and cut away excess fabric underneath.

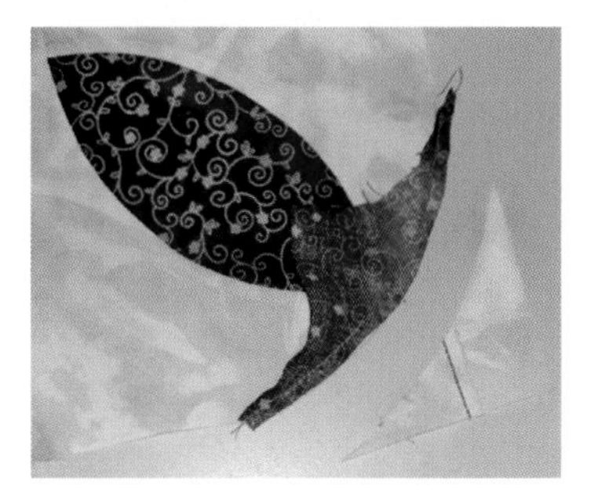

Freezer Paper Template

8. Trim away excess block fabric, press and trim outside edges.

Bending Bows

56" x 56" Sewn by Elisa Wilson and Quilted by Linda Noort.

Harvest Table Runner

Only three blocks are used in this table runner. Each block is set on point. A great way to use up your extra blocks. You could change the fabric and make one for each season of the year.

Materials and Cutting

- 1/8 yard for center melon – Cut 3 of shape B.
- 1/3 yard for A and C shape – Cut 3 of shape A and C.
- 1/8 yard or scraps for corner triangles – Cut 12 – 3 ½" squares.
- ½ yard for setting triangles – Cut 6 – 7" squares. Cut each in half.
- ½ yard for border and outside triangles – Cut 2 – 1 ½" strips and a 10 ¼" square. Cut square in half.

Sewing the Blocks

1. Sew all of the A and B shapes together.
2. Gently press seam allowance from the back, press seam away from the Melon shape. Turn block over and press from the front.
3. Sew on Piece C and press as before.
4. Refer to "Adding a Corner Piece" (page 29) and sew the 3 ½" squares onto all four sides of the three finished blocks.
5. Refer to "Setting the Block on Point" (page 33). Add setting triangles to each block.

Assembling the Quilt

1. Sew the three blocks together into a row.
2. Sew a border strip on each side.
3. Sew a border triangle on each end.

Harvest Table Runner

Sewn and quilted by Elisa Wilson. Fabric is "Mirage" from Timeless Treasures .

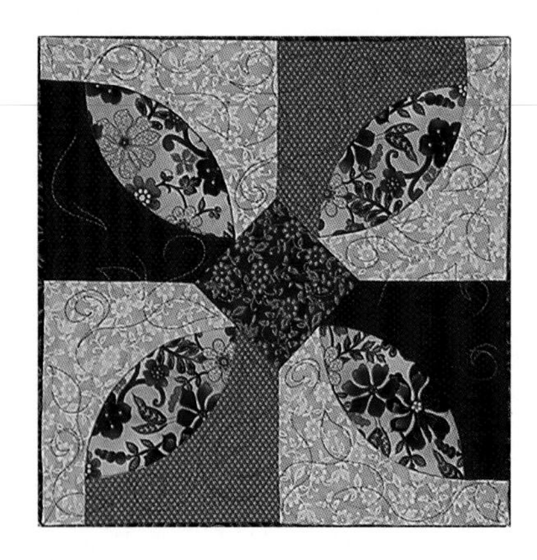

Perennial Path

Materials

- 1 ½ yards Light
- ¾ yard Green
- ½ yard each from two different Yellows
- ¼ yard Orange
- ½ yard Floral
- 3 yards Backing
- ½ yard Binding

Cutting

- 10 of shape A from each Yellow for a total of 20
- 20 of shape C from the Light
- 20 of shape B from the Floral
- 20 – 3 ½" squares from the Orange
- 8 – 9" squares from the Green
- 8 – 9" squares from the Light

Sewing the Blocks

1. Sew all of the A and B shapes together.
2. Gently press seam allowance from the back, press seam away from the Melon shape. Turn block over and press from the front.
3. Sew on Piece C. Press again as above.
4. Sew on one corner square. Refer to "Adding a Corner Piece" (page 29)
5. Place the green and light 9" fabric squares right sides together. Draw a diagonal line on the wrong side of the fabric. Sew ¼" along each side of the diagonal line. Cut apart on the line.
6. Open each half-square triangle block and press. Trim to 8 ½". You will need 16 of these blocks.

Assembling the Quilt

1. Sew 4 of the Melon blocks together to resemble a flower.
2. Sew 4 of the half-square triangle blocks together as shown in the picture.
3. Assemble these new blocks together in 3 horizontal rows of 3. Sew blocks together into rows. Press the seams in opposite directions from row to row.
4. Sew rows together.

Perennial Path

48" x 48" Sewn by Elisa Wilson, quilted by Linda Noort.
Fabric is "Mirage" by Timeless Treasures .

Watermelon Wedge

This table topper is the perfect accent for a summer picnic table. The centers look like cool, crisp watermelon and fusible bias tape is used to make the rinds.

Materials

- One package ¼" fusible bias tape in Dark Green
- ½ yard total of assorted Watermelon Reds
- 1 ¼ yard total of assorted Background fabrics
- ¾ yard Green

Cutting

Red

- 6 – 2 ½" strips
  Sew together into pairs. Press seam open.
  From these strip sets cut 12 of shape B.

Background

- 12 of shape A and C
- 4 – 8 ½" squares

Green

- 6 – 1 ½" strips for sashing
  Sub-cut 3 of the strips into 12 – 8 ½" segments.
- 5 – 2 ½" strips for binding

Sewing the Blocks

1. Sew all of the A and B shapes together.
2. Gently press seam allowance from the back, press seam away from the Melon shape. Turn block over and press from the front.
3. Sew on shape C and press again as above.

Assembling the Quilt

1. Lay out the blocks and sashing pieces. You will use the 8 ½" squares during the assembly and the corners can be cut after the piece is quilted.
2. Sew the blocks together with the sashing pieces in-between the blocks to make 4 rows.
3. Sew the row together with the longer sashing pieces.
4. Quilt the top and cut the corners at a 45° angle before adding binding.
5. Place ¼" fusible binding around theMelon shapes. Top stitch through binding and all the layers of the quilt.

Watermelon Wedge

35" x 35" Sewn by Elisa Wilson and quilted by Linda Noort.
Hand dyed fabric is by Sue at Abeo Designs.

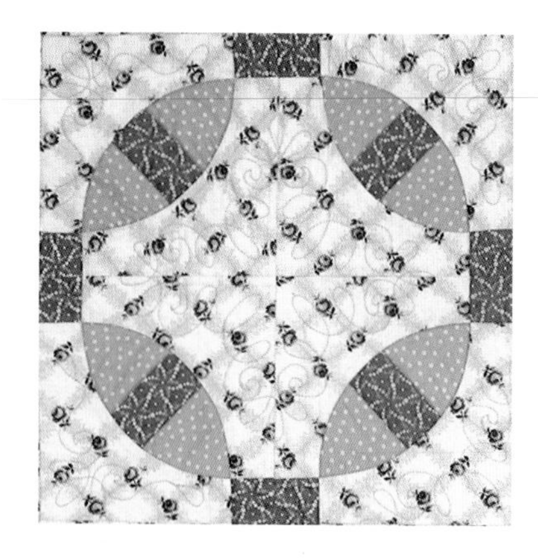

Wedding Bells

A larger version of this quilt would showcase a full sized bed just beautifully. I wanted to make this quilt bigger but I ran out of fabric and time. This Wedding Ring concept turns out just perfect. You will be using only the A shape for the background in this block.

Materials

- 1 ¼ yards Light for background
- 1 yard Blue for Melon
- ¼ yard Purple for stripe & corner square
- 5/8 yard for Border
- ½ yard for Binding
- 2 yards for Backing

Cutting

Blue Melon

- 4 – 4" strips for center Melon
- 4 – 4 ½" squares for border

Purple

- 2 – 2" strips for center Melon
- 2 – 2" strips – Sub-cut 32 – 2" squares

Background

- 32 – shape A

Border

- 4- 4 ½" strips

Sewing the Blocks

1. Sew a Blue 4" strip onto each side of the Purple 2" strip. Press seams in.
2. Center Melon shape B over this and cut out 16.
3. Sew 16 shape A's to the Melon shape B. Gently press seam allowance from the back, press seam away from the melon shape. Turn block over and press from the front.
4. Sew the 2" squares onto the ends of the remaining 16 shape A's. Refer to "Adding a Corner Square" (page 31). Press seams in.
5. Sew the A – B pieces to the shapes made in step 4. Press seams as before.

Assembling the Quilt

1. Place blocks in 4 horizontal rows of 4 blocks each.
2. Sew blocks together into rows. Press the seams in opposite directions from row to row.
3. Sew rows together.
4. Measure and cut the 4 border strips to the width of the quilt.

5. Sew the Purple 4 ½" squares on the ends of two of these strips. Sew on the border strips. Refer to "Sewing on Borders" (page 83).

Wedding Bells

40" x 40" Sewn by Elisa Wilson, quilted by Linda Noort.
Fabric is "Champagne Gardens" by Marcus Brothers .

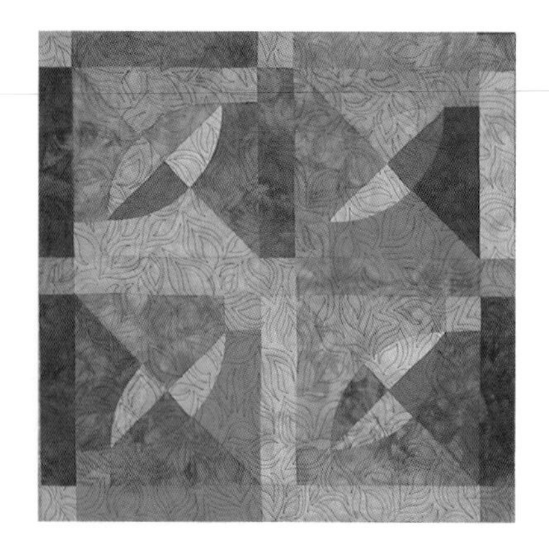

Good & Fruity

I began with a fat quarter packet of 18 fabrics in pastel rainbow colors. First I sorted four of the blue shades and four of the yellowish shades and used those for the center melon shape. I sorted four of the pink shades and four of the green shades to use for the outer shape. This left me with two colors left over that I used for the corner pieces. When I started I wasn't sure how many blocks I would be able to make because I only had fat quarters. I was able to get 16 blocks and cut up the rest of the fabric into sashing. Here is the result. This will make a great baby quilt when the grandchildren start arriving.

Materials

- 18 fat quarters in a rainbow assortment; sort the fabrics into blues/ greens, yellows/oranges, and pinks/purples/reds. You will need four in each category. Use the remaining two fabrics for the corner squares and sashing squares.
- 2 yards Backing
- 1/3 yard Binding

Cutting

From the blue and the yellow fabrics –

- 2 – 2 ½" strips x 18" from each for a total of 16 strips.

From the green and pink fabrics –

- 3 – 5 ½" strips x 18" from each for a total of 24 strips.

From the remaining two fabrics –

- 32 – 2" squares.
- Cut an additional 25 – 2" squares for the sashing.

For the sashing you will use the remainder of the fabric.

- Cut 40 – 8 ½" x 2" rectangles

Sewing the blocks

1. Sew the blue and yellow 2 ½" strips together into pairs. Match up a fabric from the blue group and sew it together with a fabric from the yellow group. Press seams to one side. You will have 8 pairs.
2. Cut each set into 4 – 4 ½" segments. You will need 32 segments. Sew these segments together to make a rectangular four-patch. You will need 16.
3. Use shape B to cut out your center Melon shape from these rectangles.
4. Sew the green and pink 5 ½" strips together into pairs. Match up a fabric from the green group and the pink group. You will have 12 pairs. Press seams to one side.
5. Use shape A to cut 3 from each pair. You will need 32 of shape A.
6. Sew 16 of shape A to 16 of shape B. Press seams out.
7. On the remaining 16 of shape A you will sew a 2" square on each end.
8. Press seams in towards shape A.
9. Sew one of these onto each AB piece made in Step 6.

Assembling the Quilt

1. Use a design wall to arrange blocks in 4 horizontal rows of 4 blocks each.
2. Place sashing rectangles and remaining 2" squares in-between the blocks and around the sides of blocks.
3. Sew sashing pieces together into rows. Press seams away from 2" square.
4. Sew blocks together with sashing rectangles in-between each block. Press seams toward sashing rectangles.
5. Sew rows together.

Good & Fruity

40" x 40" Sewn by Elisa Wilson and machine quilted by Linda Noort.
Fabric is "Color Works, Sherbet" by Marcus Brothers.

Ebony & Ivory

I knew I wanted to make a black and white quilt but I wasn't sure how I wanted it to look. I played with the fabrics and made a few sample blocks before settling on this block. My daughter loves this quilt and has taken it for her own. The scrap triangles appear to float in the border.

Materials

- 4 ½ yards Black
- 3 yardsWhite
- 1 ¼ yard Red
  corner squares and binding
- 5 yards Backing

Cutting

Black

- 5 – 4 ½" strips for shape B
- 6 – 5 ½" strips for shape A
- 6 – 6 ½" strips for shape C
- 5 – 3 ½" strips of black, sub-cut 48 – 3 ½" squares. Press in half diagonally or draw a line on the back of each 3 ½" square
- 6 – 2 ½" strips of black for inner border
- 5 – 4 ½" strips for outer border

White

- 5 – 4 ½" strips for shape B
- 6 – 5 ½" strips for shape A
- 6 – 6 ½" strips for shape C

Red

- 5 – 3 ½" strips of red, sub-cut 48 – 3 ½" squares. Press in half diagonally or draw a line on the back of each 3 ½" square.

Sewing the Blocks

Template shape A –

1. Sew the 5 ½" strips together and press towards the dark. As you lay out your fabric strip make sure your dark color is on top. You will get 8 shapes from 40" of fabric. You will need 48 of shape A.

Template shape B –

2. Sew the 4 ½" strips together. Press toward the dark. You will get 11 shapes from each 40" width of fabric. You will need 48 of shape B.

Template piece C –

3. Sew together the 6 ½" strips and press towards the dark. As you lay out your fabric strip make sure your dark fabric is on the bottom. You will get 8 shapes from 40" of fabric. You will need 48 of shape C.
4. Sew all of the A and B shapes together. Align the center seams. Make sure to turn piece B so that the colors of fabric are going on opposite sides. Butt the seams together. If you pressed towards the dark both times they should be going in opposite directions and that makes this step easy.
5. Gently press seam allowance from the back, press seam away from the Melon shape. Turn block over and press from the front.
6. Sew on shape C. Press again as before.

Corner Square

7. Place a red 3 ½" square on the black corner of the completed block. Sew across the diagonal. Refer to "Adding a Corner Piece" (page 29).
8. Place a black 3 ½" square on the white corner. Sew across the diagonal.
9. Press square over. Cut away the excess ¼" from the seam allowance. SAVE THESE PIECES! You will be using them in the border.

Sewing those extra pieces

10. Chain feed those extra pieces that are cut away when adding the corner piece. They are already facing right sides together and matched up in pairs. If you feed a few in-between each pieced block you will have them sewn together in no time.
11. Press and trim each to a 2 ½" square. You will have 96 half-square triangles.
12. Alternate the black and white and the black and red half-square triangles and sew together into rows. You will need 4 rows. Two of the rows will have 20 HST in them and the other two rows will have 28 HST in them.
13. Press each row to make them flat. Set aside until border number 2 is needed.

Assembling the Quilt

1. Take four blocks and sew them together to make one large block. Be careful with your placement of color. You will be making 12 of these new blocks.

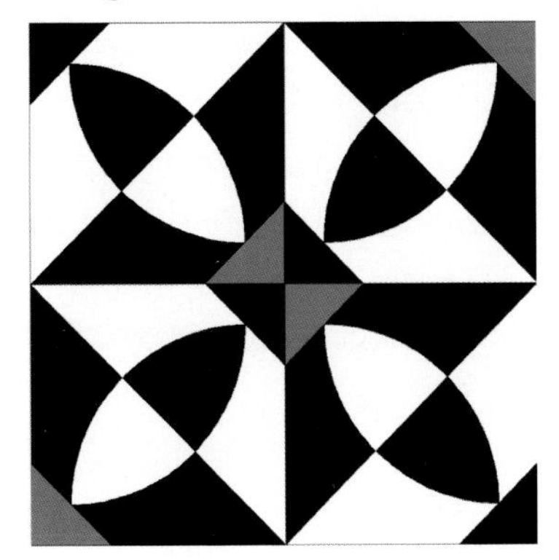

2. Sew these blocks together in 4 horizontal rows of 3- 16" blocks each. Your quilt top should measure approximately 48 ½" x 64 ½".
3. Refer to "Sewing on Borders" (page 83). In this quilt you will sew the first and second border together before sewing onto the quilt. Measure and cut 2 strips for the 1st border.

Alternative Settings for the blocks

4. For the second border we will use the rows of HST made earlier. To make this border fit you will need to lay out one of the longer rows of HST with the 2 ½" border strips. Use an iron to press the HST strip to make sure it is pressed flat. You want it flat but not stretched out of shape. Align the two strips together and measure the difference in length in-between the two strips. Mine was 5 ½". (Yours may be different) Add ½" for seam allowance and divide by 2. Cut two 2 ½" strips to this measurement. My two strips measured 3" each. Sew the 3" pieces onto each end of the HST row. This row should now be the same measurement as the 2 ½" strip cut in the previous step.
5. Sew these two rows together. Press seam away from the HST. Repeat for the other side.
6. Pin and sew these onto the sides of the quilt. Press seams out.
7. Repeat steps for the top and bottom inner borders. Cut two 2 ½" strips the width of the quilt top, including the two new borders. Your measurement should be approximately 56 ½". Lay out your HST strips and find the difference. Add ½" for seam allowance and divide by 2. Cut 2 – 2 ½" strips to this measurement. My two strips measured 11 ¾" each. Sew the 11 ¾" pieces onto each end of the HST row. This row should now be the same measurement as the 2 ½" strip cut in the previous step.
8. Sew these two rows together. Press seam away from the HST. Make two.
9. Pin and sew onto the top and bottom of the quit. Press seams out.
10. Refer to "Sewing on Borders" (page 83) and sew 4 ½" strips for the outside border of the quilt.

Ebony and Ivory

64" x 80" Sewn by Elisa Wilson and quilted by Linda Noort.

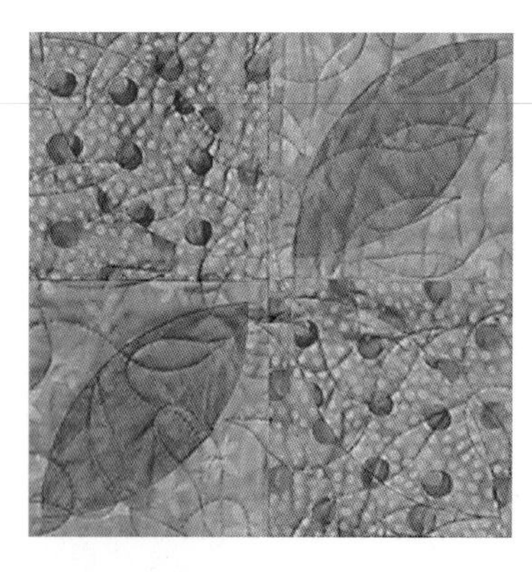

Flower Power

I wanted the Melon shape to be the predominant part of each block so after the blocks were sewn I squared each one down to 6" before sewing them together.

Materials

- 1 yard of assorted Yellows
- 1 ½ yards assorted Pinks
- 1 ½ yards assorted Greens
- ½ yard for Inner Border
- 1 yard for Outer Border
- ½ yard Binding
- 4 yards Backing

Cutting

Pink
- 18 shape A and C

Green
- 18 shape A and C

Yellow
- 36 shape B

Inner border
- 4 – 3" strips

Outer border
- 5 – 6 ½" strips

Sewing the Blocks

1. Sew all of the A and B shapes together.
2. Gently press seam allowance from the back, press seam away from the Melon shape. Turn block over and press from the front.
3. Sew on Piece C. Press seam out as above.

Assembling the Quilt

1. Use an acrylic template and square each block down to 6" square.
2. Assemble two pink background blocks and two green background blocks and sew together to make a new flower block.
3. Assemble the new flower blocks together into 3 horizontal rows of 3 each.
4. Sew the blocks together into rows. Press the seams in opposite directions from row to row.
5. Sew the rows together.
6. Refer to "Sewing on Borders" (page 83) and sew on the inner and outer borders.

Flower Power

53" x 53" Sewn by Elisa Wilson and quilted by Linda Noort.
Fabrics are by Free Spirit.

Indian Summer

The center of this block was cut from two different fabrics but rather than aligning the center seam to keep it straight it was purposefully cut at an angle. The illusion you get is of leaves of different colors. The blocks were cut slightly smaller so that the center of the block was more prominent. Only twenty blocks are used in this quit.

Materials

Use a variety of autumn colors for the blocks.

- 5 half yards in a variety of greens and browns
- 7 fat quarters in yellows and oranges
- ¼ yard for outer border 1
- ⅓ yard for outer border 2
- ⅝ yard for outer border 3
- 3 yards backing
- ½ yard binding

Cutting

Greens and Browns

- 20 of each shape A and C
- 4 – 2" strips for inner border

Yellows

- 14 – 2 ½" x 22" strips for Shape B
- 4- 1 ¼" x 22" for Inner Border

Outer Borders

- Outer border 1 – cut 4 – 1 ¼" strips
- Outer border 2 – cut 4 – 2" strips
- Outer border 3 – cut 5 – 3 ½" strips

Sewing the Blocks

1. Randomly sew the yellow and orange 2 ½" strips together and press seams to one side. Make 7 pairs.
2. Place template B at an angle on these strips and out 20 of shape B. You should get 3 from each pair.
3. Sew all of the A and B shapes together.
4. Gently press seam allowance from the back, press seam away from the Melon shape. Turn block over and press from the front.
5. Sew on Piece C. Press seam out as above.
6. Trim each block to 7 ½" square.

Assembling the Quilt

1. Sew 4 blocks together to make the center.
2. Sew a 1 ¼" yellow and 2 - 2" green border strips together. Yellow is in the center with a green strip on each side. Make 4 and cut to 18". Measure your center and add 4 ¼" to make sure of this measurement.
3. Sew one of these inner border sets to the center blocks. Start at one end but do not sew completely to the other end. You will have a tail of inner border strip left hanging. This will be sewn on last.

4. Press seam allowance out and sew on another border strip, start at the center block and sew to the end of the finished side of the first border strip. Continue around the quilt with the remaining two inner border sets.
5. After the last inner border set is sewn on come back and complete the sewing of the first border set.
6. Sew together 2 rows of 3 blocks. Sew one of these on each side of the quilt.
7. Sew together 2 rows of 5 blocks. Sew one of these on the top and bottom of the quilt top.
8. Outer Border. Refer to "Sewing on Borders" (page 83). You will have 3 border strips to sew on. Start with outer border 1 which is 1 ¼" wide and continue with outer border 2 and then outer border 3.

Indian Summer

46" x 46" Sewn by Elisa Wilson, quilted by Linda Noort.
Fabric used is "Artisan's Palette" from Northcott Silk .

The Brakeman's Lantern

This quilt was named to honor those who worked to build the railways in the mid-nineteenth century. I've not seen a block like this authentic to that time period but if our foremothers would have had this template and a rotary cutter, I'll bet they would have made one just like this. Quilt and pattern by Mary Lucille.

Materials

- 5/8 yard each of 16 assorted light, medium and dark prints
- 2 ½ yards of a lengthwise stripe fabric for "the strips"
- 1 ¼ yard dark for sides of strips and binding
- 5/8 yard medium for accent triangles used in Step 7

Cutting

From EACH your 16 assorted prints cut

- 2 of each A, B and C shape. You will have a total of 32 of each shape.
- 4 – 9 ¼" squares-Cut each square in half diagonally. Alternate the direction of your cuts. This will keep any directional fabrics such as plaids or stripes properly aligned. Use for Setting Triangles in Step 5.
- 4 – 3 ½" squares, draw a line or press in half diagonally. Use for corner triangles on blocks.

Stripe fabric – Cut LENGTHWISE

- 5 – 6" x 90" strips

Dark

- 18 – 1" strips for Step 9
- 8 – 2 ½" strips for binding

Medium Accent Triangles

- 64 – 3 ½" squares. Draw a line or press in half diagonally. Use in setting triangles in Step 7.

Sewing the Blocks

1. Sew all of the A and B shapes together.
2. Gently press seam allowance from the back, press seam away from the Melon shape. Turn block over and press from the front.
3. Sew on shape C. Shape C will be the same fabric as shape A in each block.
4. Place a 3 ½" square on two corners of the block at the point of the melon B shape, right sides together. Sew on the line. Press and trim. Refer to "Adding a Corner Piece" (page 29). For each block use the same corner triangle fabric that you use for the Melon shape.
5. Lay out your blocks in vertical rows in a pleasing combination of 4 rows of 8 blocks. Place the setting triangle pieces of your choice around each block. Take some time with this so you get the distribution just the way you want it.
6. Sew the adjoining setting triangles together into pairs.

7. To these setting triangle sets, you will be sewing on an additional accent triangle. Add the medium corner triangle squares at the end using the same method as in Step 4.
8. The rows of blocks must be assembled diagonally. After the row is assembled you may wish to go back and trim any excess to give you a ¼" seam allowance along the long edge. Set aside.

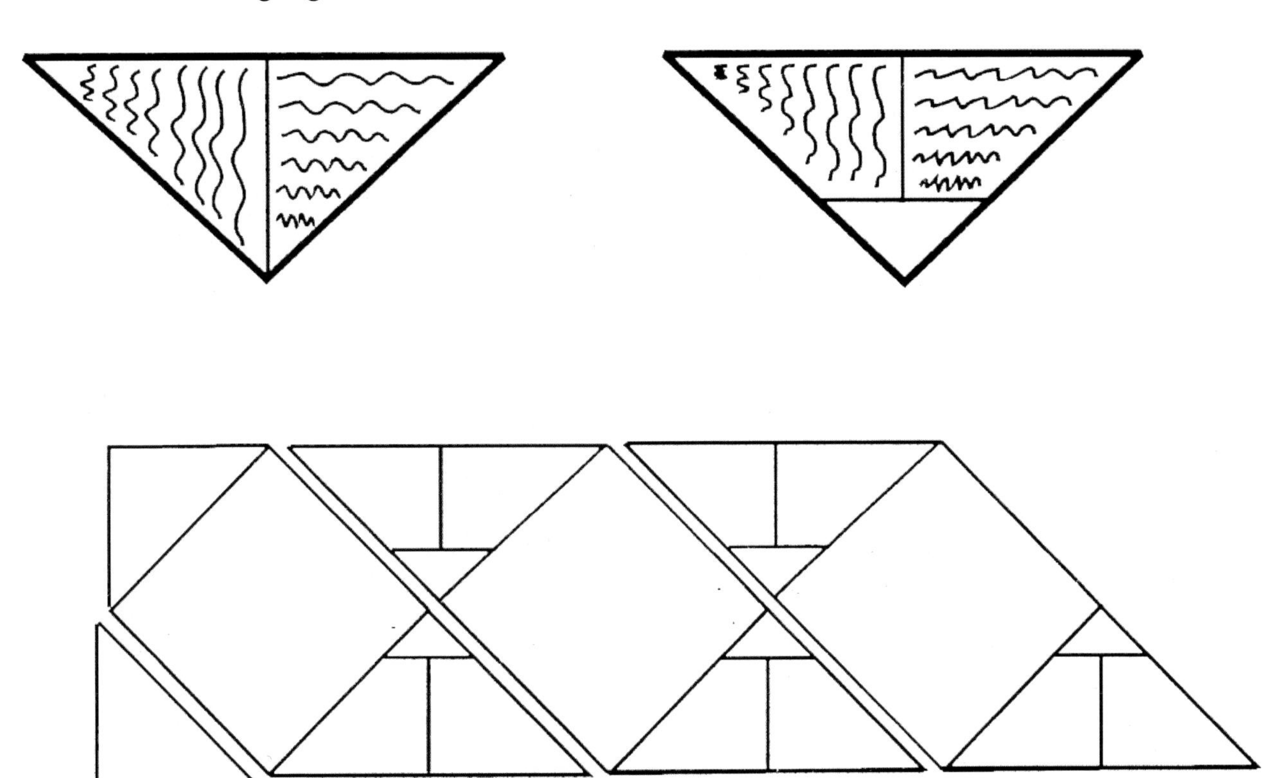

9. Sew the 1" dark fabric strips together end to end as you would binding to make one long continuous strip. Cut into 8 – 90" strips.
10. Sew a 1" dark strip to both left and right long sides of 3 of the Stripe fabric strips.
11. Sew a 1" dark strip to one side of the two remaining Stripe fabric strips. If your stripe fabric is directional be sure you are sewing the dark strip on the correct side.

Assembling the Quilt

1. You are now ready to assemble the long rows into your quilt top. Start with a Stripe fabric with one dark edge; on the right side add a row of blocks then a Stripe fabric set with two black edges. Continue two more times with another Stripe fabric set with two dark edges and then add the remaining Stripe fabric set with the one black edge.

The Brakeman's Lantern

79" x 96" Sewn by Mary Lucille and machine quilted by Kittrell Strunc.
A variety of antique reproduction fabrics were used.

Sewing on Borders

Borders are best added by first measuring the length and width in the center of the quilt.

The outside edges of a quilt can become slightly longer because of stretching that happens during the handling of the quilt.

I prefer to add my border strips by first cutting of the selvage and then sewing the fabric strips together, end to end. Press the seams open or in one direction.

I lay out the quilt top on my cutting table if it will fit and smooth it flat without stretching it. I then lay my strips along the center of this and smooth them without stretching. Then I use my rotary cutter and cut two strips this size.

While I am still at the cutting table I can pin both sides of the border. Match each end and ease any difference over the length of the border. Pin in the center and then every 8" to 10".

Sew both of these borders and press the seam out. Lay the quilt the other direction on the cutting table and measure two more strips for the remaining two sides of the quilt.

If my cutting table is too small I will lay the quilt on a hard surface floor. I bring a cutting mat to slide under the edge of the quilt where I will be cutting the border strip.

Some borders are cut to the exact width and length of the quilt top. A corner piece is added to the length or width and the borders are sewn on in the same manner.

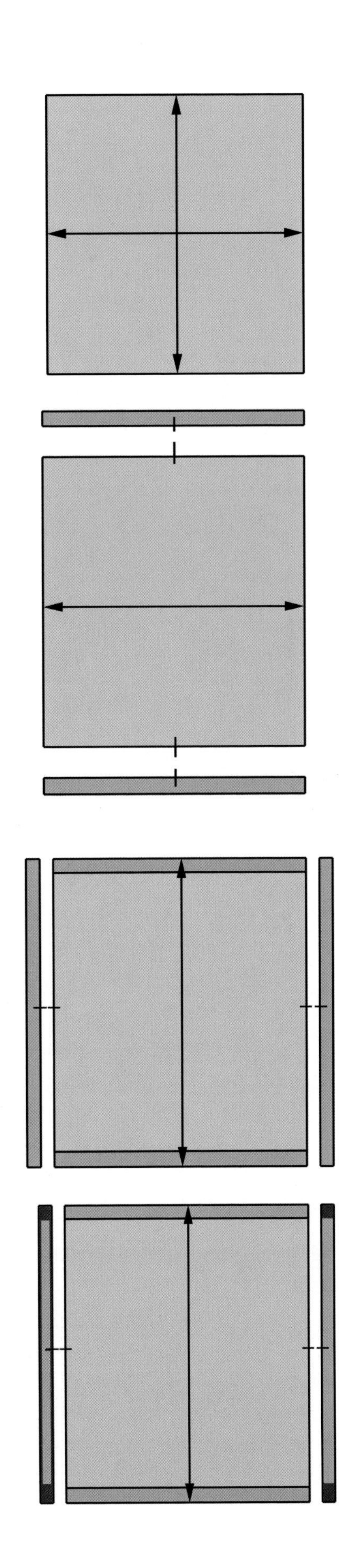

TheBack side

The back of your quilt doesn't have to be boring. Here are a few of my favorite backing tips.

- Choose a light colored fabric and quilt with a darker or variegated thread. This gives you a reversible quilt. This would also work well with a dark fabric and a lighter thread color.

- You probably have a lot of fat quarters in your stash right? Why buy extra yardage for the back. Sew them together for a patchwork look that is easy and fun to look at.

- If you don't have enough fat quarters but you do have leftover fabric from your project you can piece it together to make an interesting back. Throw in an extra block or two.

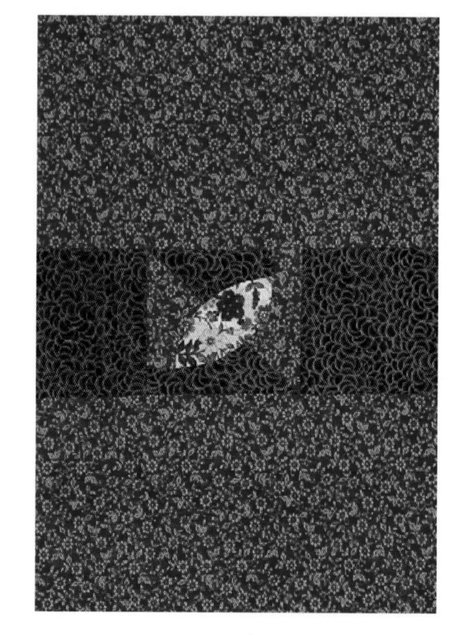

- If you want to use just one fabric on the back make sure it is something that you really love. Maybe a favorite fabric that you didn't want to cut up.

- Add an extra block to the back to use as a label. Sew into place on a pieced back with your extra fabric.

- Make sure to sign your quilt.

Binding

Binding directions are based on cutting 2 1/2" strips and using a 3/8" seam allowance.
Sew your binding strips end to end to make one long continuous strip.
Press in half lengthwise, wrong sides together. Roll the binding into a coil until ready to use.

1. Start sewing about 10" from the top. Leave a 3" tail of binding.
2. Stop sewing 3/8" away from the end. Fold binding up so that it is parallel with right side of quilt.
3. Fold binding down along the right side of the quilt. Make sure your fold is even with the top edge of the quilt. Continue around the quilt.
4. When you are about 3" away from where you started, stop sewing and leave an additional 3" tail.
5. Lay the upper ending strip right side up. Lay the lower binding strip on top, right sides together. Draw a diagonal line and sew together on this line.
6. Trim seam allowance. Press seam open. Fold in half lengthwise and press again. Sew this binding to the quilt. Press binding over and machine or hand stitch binding down.

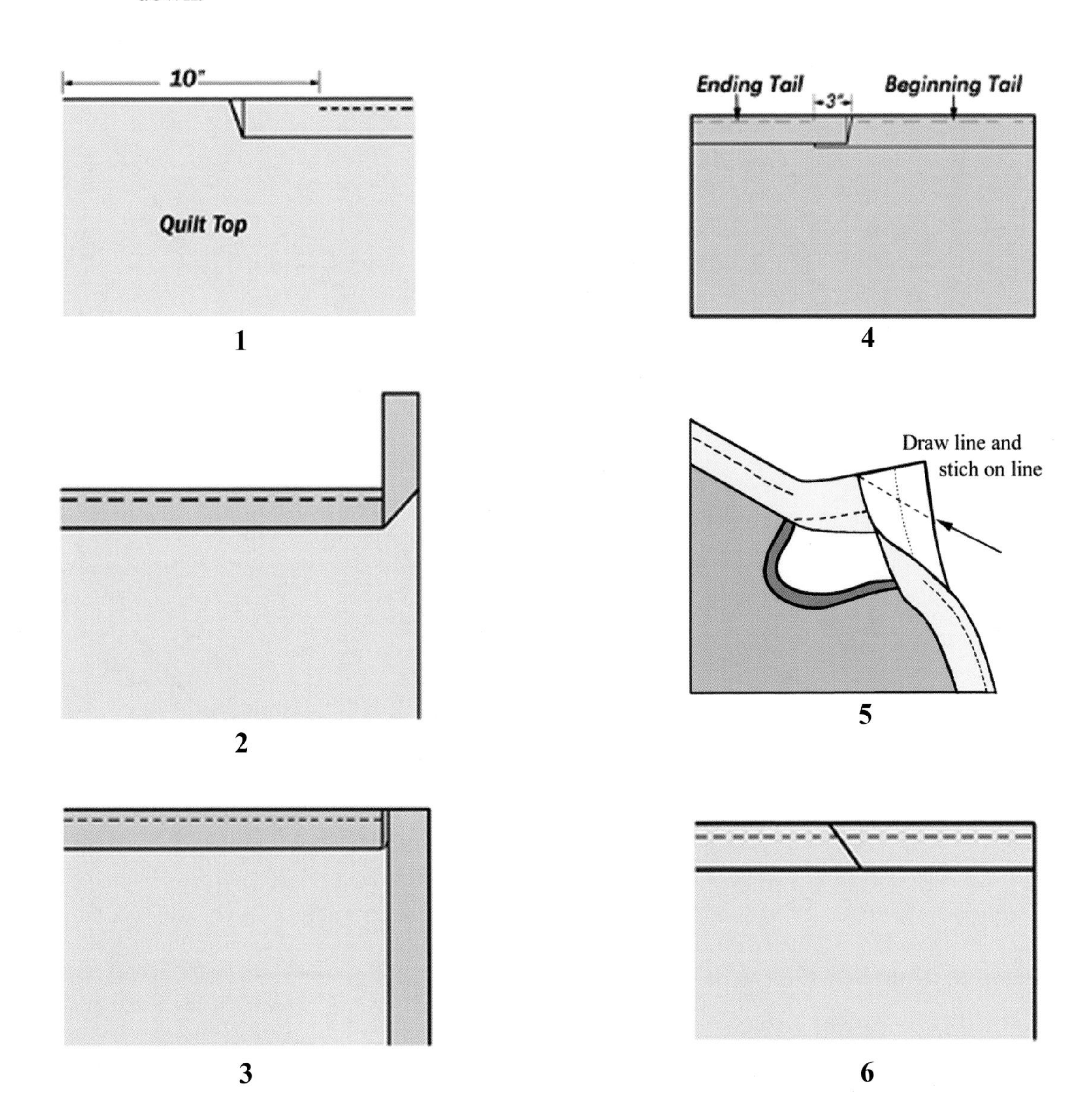

Templates

The templates for the projects are here for you to trace and includes the ¼" seam allowance.

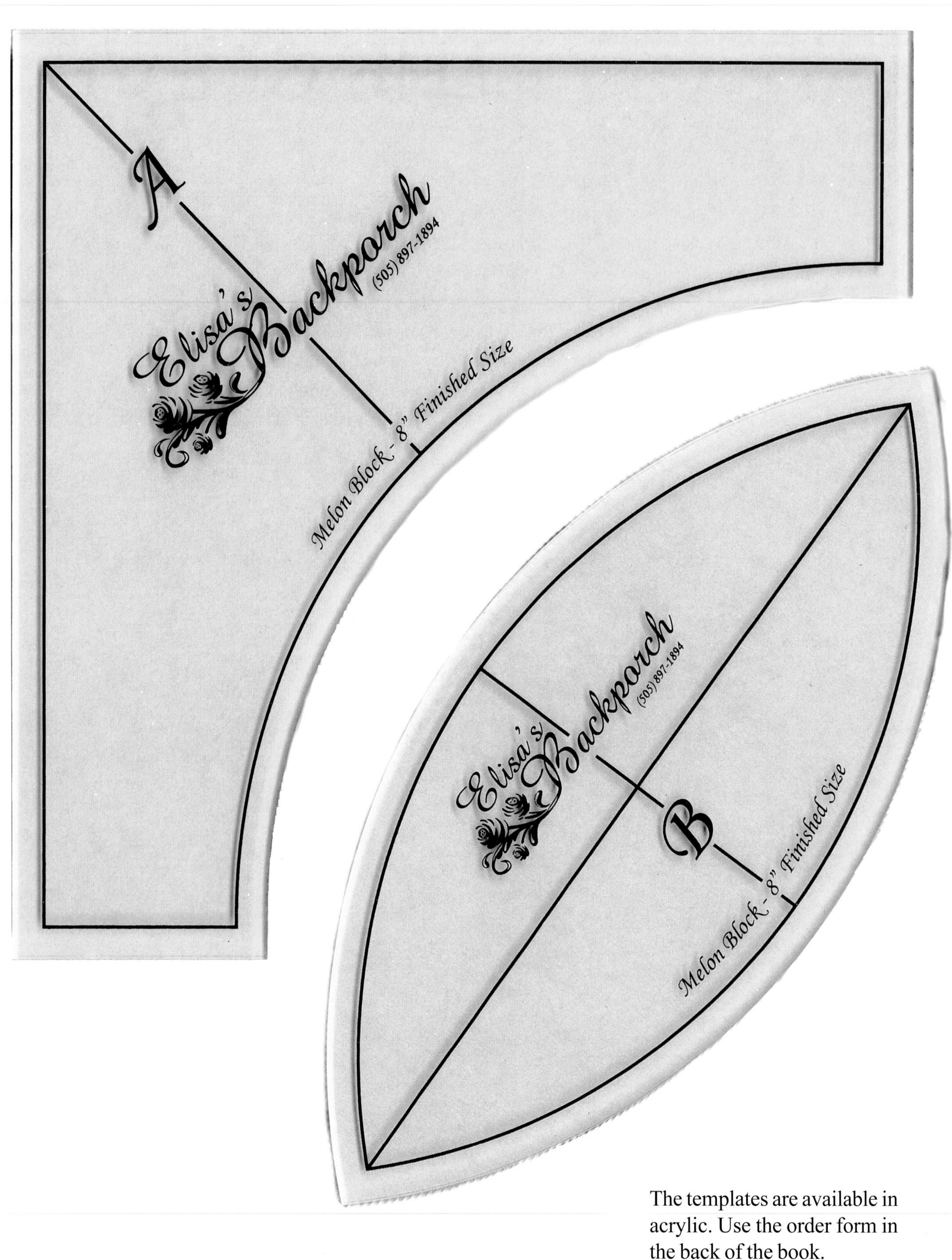

The templates are available in acrylic. Use the order form in the back of the book.

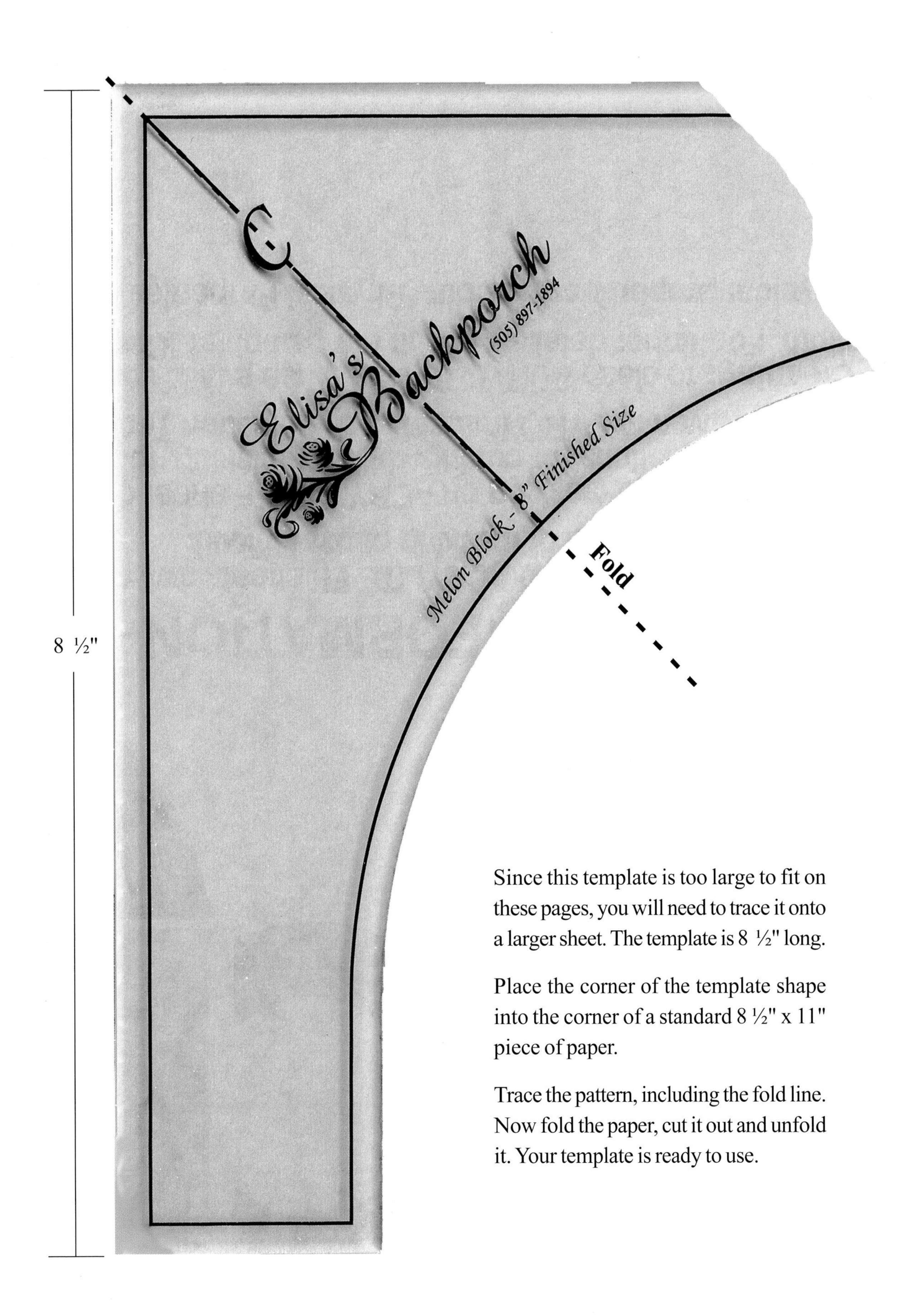

Since this template is too large to fit on these pages, you will need to trace it onto a larger sheet. The template is 8 ½" long.

Place the corner of the template shape into the corner of a standard 8 ½" x 11" piece of paper.

Trace the pattern, including the fold line. Now fold the paper, cut it out and unfold it. Your template is ready to use.

Quilt Gallery

The quilts in this gallery were all sewn by Amber Peterson. She was given the Melon Block template to test and she came up with all of these beautiful quilts. They are all her own design. Photo's by Pat Barrett.

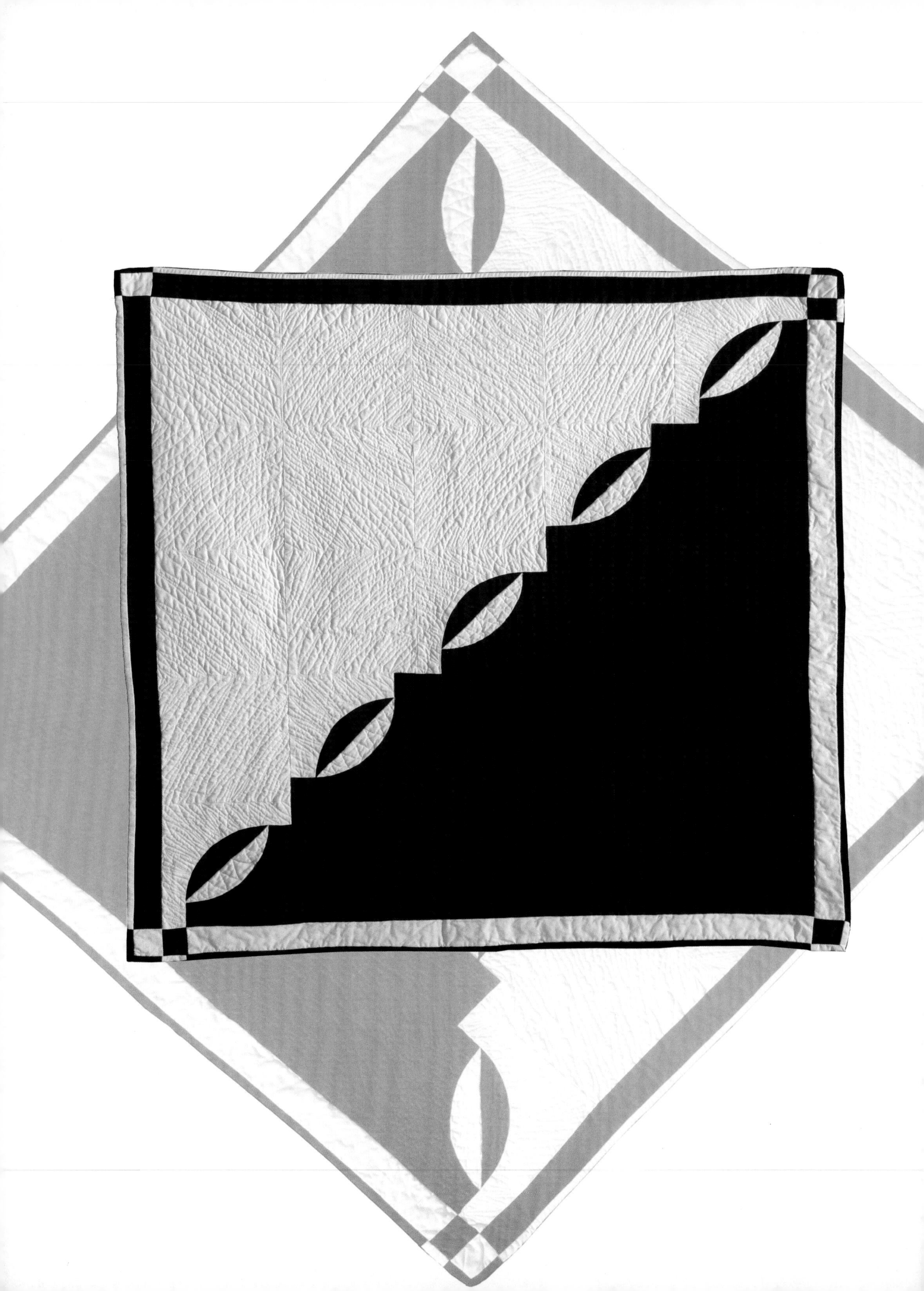

About the author

Elisa lives in the Land of Enchantment, New Mexico that is, with her husband and two of their three children. The writing of this book along with the designing and sewing of all the quilts took place in the midst of a wedding, a move and a major remodeling of their house. The cutting mat shared the same space as the temporary kitchen in the midst of hanging drywall, plumbing and electrical messes. By the time this book is at the printer the building of the new studio will still be in progress. What a glorious day its completion will be.

Elisa's love of color and creative imagination leads her to come up with many ideas based upon the same design. Before she has even completed one idea she has started three or four more. This leads to a never ending supply of projects begging to be finished.

In 2003 Elisa's first book *Crazy Curves* was published and continues to be popular among quilters across the country. Curves really aren't that difficult and they lead to so many more ideas just waiting to be tried.

Quilter's Notes

Quilter's Notes

Order Form

Ship to:
Name ____________________

Address ____________________

City ____________________ State__________ Zip__________

Phone (required for FedEx)____________________ Email____________________

Qty	Item	Cost	Total
	Melon Block Template	$ 22.95	
	Additional *Melon Block* Book	$ 24.95	
	Other books and templates		
	Crazy Curves Book	$ 21.95	
	3 ½" Small Paths Template Set	$ 9.95	
	7" Crazy Curves Template Set	$ 12.95	
	4" Drunkard's Path Template Set	$ 10.95	
	8" Rainbow Template Set	$ 21.95	
	Shipping ($ 4.50 one item, $ 1.00 each additional item)		
	New Mexico Residents add 6.75% sales tax		
	Total		

☐ Check ☐ Credit Card Master Card Visa

Credit Card # ____________________ Exp. Date__________

Signature ____________________

Shipping
One Item…………....$ 4.50
$ 1.00 for each additional item.
US prices only.
Please call for out of country shipping prices.

Mail order with payment to:
Elisa's Backporch Inc.
1200 Forest Road NW
Albuquerque, NM 87114
(505) 897-1894
Fax (505) 792-9371
www.backporchdesign.com

Products available from Elisa's Backporch or at your local quilt store.

Quilt shop owners – You can carry these products in your store.

Order direct or call for a current list of distributors.